Family Child Care

Marketing Guide

How to Build Enrollment and Promote Your
Business As a Child Care Professional

by Tom Copeland, J.D.

Redleaf Press

Published by: Redleaf Press
                a division of Resources for Child Caring
                450 North Syndicate, Suite 5
                St. Paul, MN 55104

Printed in the United States of America

ISBN: 1-884834-75-2

Policy on duplication and distribution of materials in this book:
Examples from the Appendix may be copied and used in business by the owner of
this book. Additionally, trainers may secure permission to use examples of the
Appendix in course materials by calling Redleaf Press, 651-641-6664.

        Library of Congress Cataloging-in-Publication Data

Copeland, Tom.
        Family child care marketing guide : how to build enrollment and promote your business
as a child care professional / Tom Copeland.
        p.   cm.
        Includes bibliographic references and index.
        ISBN 1-884834-75-2
        1. Family day care—United States—Marketing. 2 Child care services—United
States—Marketing. I. Title.
        HQ778.63 .C66 1999
        362.71'2'0688—dc21   CIP
                                                                        99-051510

Acknowledgments

Thanks to the following people for providing valuable feedback and suggestions for this book: Joe Perreault, family child care advocate; Robert Sullivan, Loudoun County Department of Social Service; Sue and Warren Schmidt, Monday Morning America, Inc.; Gershia Coggs, Data Base Inc.; Sue Molstad, Resources for Child Caring; Gail Birch, Provider's Choice Food Program; Diane Phillippi, Ramsey County Family Day Care Licensing Unit; Denise Lane-Porter, Building Blocks Tax Service; Thorton Lam, Child Nutrition, Inc.; Andrea Howlett, Crystal Stairs Food Program; Beverly C. Samuel, Virginia Cooperative Extension; family child care providers Nora Laagard, Grace Emery, Sandy Governor, Beth Mork, Adela Rojas, Lynn Manfredi/Petitt, Peggy Haack; and Reva Wywadis, regional representative of the National Association for Family Child Care. Thanks also to Redleaf Press staff: Dan Verdick, Alyn Bedford, Anne Holzman, Paul Woods, Eileen Nelson, Susan Firestone, and Teina Rowell, and to illustrator Melissa Muldoon.

Redleaf National Institute
The National Center for the Business of Family Child Care

Redleaf National Institute's mission is to improve the quality of family child care by delivering high-quality products and services that strengthen the ability of providers to successfully manage their business. The Institute offers training, telephone assistance, a Web site, and help in handling IRS audits. Tom Copeland is the director of the Institute.

The Institute offers provider training workshops on record keeping, tax preparation, contracts and policies, marketing, and other legal and business issues. It also conducts a workshop entitled "Teaching Family Child Care Record Keeping and Tax Preparation." This workshop is for trainers, tax preparers, and those who assist providers.

The Institute's Web site is www.redleafinstitute.org. This Web site contains

- Provider Business News—The latest tax and business information affecting providers.
- Ask the Institute—Your opportunity to ask questions and have them answered on-line.

- Training Services—Details about the Institute's training schedule and how to bring a workshop to your area.
- Tax Preparer Directory—A listing of tax preparers by state who have experience preparing family child care tax returns.
- Business Library—Posting of IRS publications, Tax Court cases, business articles, handouts, and other business information.
- Redleaf Press—Descriptions of the latest books published by Redleaf Press.
- Marketing Tips—We will post ways that other providers have adapted and succeeded with the ideas presented in this book.

Table of Contents

CHAPTER ONE

Introduction to Family Child Care Marketing

The Profession of Family Child Care

Family child care is a profession. It is a unique profession that requires a wide variety of skills: teacher, protector, cook, chauffeur, bookkeeper, organizer, and much, much more. It is a job that hundreds of thousands of women and men perform because they love children and they want to support their own family. When we talk about a family child care professional, we are not referring to a babysitter. A babysitter is someone who watches children (usually from just one family) for a few hours in the evening while the parents are away from home at a movie or social event. A family child care provider is someone who is in the business of teaching and nurturing young children to reach their highest potential, usually for more than 50 hours a week, year-round. A provider is intentional about planning activities and helping meet the individual, changing needs of the children in care. This is no easy job.

At its heart, family child care is about the very personal relationship between a caregiver, a child, and the child's family. This home-centered, personal relationship is what makes family child care so special. At the same time, providers must also care for their own physical and emotional needs in order to be able to continue offering this unique service. In the long run, providers must learn to balance the personal and business side of their profession to be successful.

Being a family child care professional means being in control of your business. You are responsible for setting your own rates and hours, and deciding who your customers will be and what type of curriculum you will offer. Before you care for your first child, you should decide what kind of business you want to have. This is one of the best parts of being self-employed. You are the boss! You are free to set your own rules (with the narrow exception of illegal-discrimination laws) and change them whenever you want. Because of this, you should make choices that will make you happy. It doesn't make sense to set up your business, successfully market it to customers, and then quit a year later because you were unhappy with how little you made, or because you didn't like the fact that you had no paid vacation time. If you have been in business for a few years and haven't thought carefully about what you want, it is never too late to do so. Once you have defined what you want as a business, marketing becomes a very powerful ally for you. If you are not in control of your business, marketing it will not make things better.

This book focuses on family child care marketing. Although it discusses marketing in business language (**finder's fee,** promotions, competition, and so on), providers should understand that there is no contradiction between offering a high-quality home-based program and marketing it as a business. In fact, a comprehensive national study about the quality of family child care concluded that providers are more likely to rank higher on objective measures of quality if they follow standard business practices and charge higher rates! (See "The Study of Children in Family Child Care and Relative Care" as cited in the Appendix.)

Nothing in this book should be taken to mean that to be successful marketers of their businesses, providers must adopt negative business trappings such as cutthroat competition, high-pressure sales tactics, the worship of bigger and bigger profits, or a win-lose mentality. We believe that all providers can achieve success in marketing their business while keeping the casual, homey, friendly, warm, and professional aspects of their program.

We recognize that for some providers, marketing their business presents special challenges. We live in a society where discrimination based on race, sex, religion, class, disability, sexual orientation, and ethnic background still exists. In addition, a limited educational background or lack of access to support agencies and community services can sometimes, but not always, create barriers to success for providers. This book does not attempt to offer answers to how providers can overcome these barriers of discrimination and lack of opportunity. We do believe that all family child care providers can exercise a measure of pride and control over how they run their own business by following some of the ideas presented in this book.

What Is Family Child Care Marketing?

Simply stated, family child care marketing is how you communicate the benefits of your program to parents who might use your services. Many family child care providers think that marketing is advertising. It is much more. Marketing is

- Defining your service (How is my program meeting the needs of children and parents?)

- Pricing your service (What is my time worth?)
- Promoting your service (How do I tell others about my program?)

This book will cover all of these points and more.

The goal of marketing is to reach parents and compel them to purchase your services. To do this you need to focus on meeting the needs of parents and their children. Parents want a safe, high-quality provider for their children that will enable them to work and support their family. Providers must keep the needs of parents and children foremost in their minds. This book will help you identify the needs of parents and children and how you can meet them.

Many providers think about marketing only when they have an opening to fill. Marketing is not something to do just when you're starting your business or when you have an opening. It is not something to stop doing once you have a waiting list, because one or more of your families could leave without notice. It should be conducted every year you are in business. Successful marketing is about keeping your current clients happy and offering the kind of care your future clients will want.

Marketing your child care program is a never-ending process. As time passes, the needs of parents change. Twenty years ago, few parents were seeking care for their infants because they stayed home to care for them. Today infant care is in great demand because of the tremendous increase in single-parent and dual-career families. It is important to keep up with changing needs in the child care field so your program will be successful in the future. This means asking a lot of questions of other individuals and organizations that can help you market your program. We will show you how to work with other organizations and individuals such as **Child Care Resource and Referral agencies, child care regulators, competitors**, employers, and more in chapter 7.

Marketing and the Quality of Child Care

Operating a high-quality child care program is the foundation of all your marketing efforts. You may be able to attract parents to your program through your promotional efforts, but without a quality program you won't be able to keep them. Many family child care providers go out of business each year, in large part because they weren't offering high-quality care. Providers who use this book should always keep in mind that what they are marketing is their high-quality program, not their house, their backyard, or their computer. A high-quality program means child-centered activities, nutritious meals, individual care, and a safe, homey environment run by a trained caregiver. Part of your marketing job is to help educate parents about what high-quality child care looks like. (See the Skills list in the Appendix.) Chapter 2 describes how to identify and communicate the benefits of your program so parents will understand why they should enroll their child with you.

derstand that a high-quality program also includes paying
 environment and what you need to be able to run a stable busi-
e consistent care children need. Work environment issues include
acations, holidays, and sick days, backup help, regular profes-
t training, written contracts and policies, and more. The Center for
orkforce has developed model work standards for family child care
ther Resources in the Appendix.

Future Trends in the Child Care Field

The child care field has experienced tremendous change in the last 20 years, and it will likely undergo significant changes in the future. In the last few years studies have shown that the percentage of children enrolling in regulated family child care homes has declined slowly while the percentage of children enrolling in child care centers, as well as in unregulated in-home care, is growing. In part, this is due to the failure of providers to use the power of marketing to promote their profession. What are some trends we might expect to see? Although it is largely a matter of guesswork, here are some possible trends that will affect your program:

- Competition from other child care programs will continue to increase. There will be more regulated family child care homes, child care centers, nursery schools, employer-sponsored centers, school-age programs, and other competitors.
- There will be more competition from providers who are exempt from state regulations. These providers tend to charge lower fees.
- There will be more competition from large child care centers. These centers, often part of larger corporations or for-profit chains, will have money to spend on mass media advertising and expensive facilities.
- With expanded child care choices, parents will demand more and more from their caregivers, such as longer hours, more flexible schedules, more individual attention for their child, or access to new technology. If one program won't meet their needs, parents will be more likely to leave and enroll in another program.
- There will be a greater demand for more specialized child care services: sick care, drop-in care, weekend and evening care, care for children with a wide range of physical and mental abilities, and more. It will become harder and harder to operate a program that serves only preschoolers, Monday through Friday, 7 A.M. to 6 P.M.
- As competition grows, more child care programs will close down because of financial pressures. Most family child care providers operate with a very small profit. With few expenses to cut, any loss of enrollment will quickly create a financial emergency. Providers will have to learn how to plan for the ups and downs of enrollment.

- It will take longer to fill child care openings. This means providers will have to spend more time and money on advertising and promoting their program.
- Child care programs that have good business skills and the ability to communicate with parents will be more likely to succeed.
- Although the overall demand for child care will continue to grow slowly, the greatest growth in the population of children under the age of six will be from children of non-Caucasian origin.
- There will be more children in child care from single-parent households.
- There will be an increase in the number of family child care associations, networks, and support groups. Those not a part of these groups will find it more difficult to be visible to potential customers.
- More parents will be looking for objective standards of quality when they are choosing a child care program. They will want programs that can demonstrate that they are educating their children.
- Welfare reform is here to stay. Its impact on family child care could be contradictory. In some states it will mean more government regulations such as training requirements. In other states it may undermine existing regulations.

These trends indicate why marketing is so important to family child care providers. Because providers operate out of private homes and are largely invisible to parents, they have a special challenge when they try to market their program. Child care centers and school-age programs operate out of clearly identifiable buildings and storefronts that are easy to find. This book will help providers to be a little more creative than their competition and thus become more visible to parents.

Getting Started

What if you wanted to become a family child care provider but knew absolutely nothing about running a family child care business? How would you begin to find out what you needed to know to be successful? Here are the first steps you should probably take:

1) Find out what parents want from their child care provider. Talk to parents who now use child care or are looking for child care.
2) Identify who are the best providers in your area and meet with them to learn how they do it. Ask a provider to be your mentor. Volunteer to work in another provider's home for a few days.
3) Approach the organizations that work with providers and ask their staff what they know about what makes a successful provider.
4) Get training in child development from a local school or through your **Child Care Resource and Referral agency.**

5) Contact your local **family child care association** and ask if you can join or at least attend the meetings.

6) Based on what you've learned, define the type of program you want to offer, describe how it will meet the needs of families, and start telling everyone about it!

We hope that this book will help you take these steps for your business. Whether you are just starting out or have been in business for many years, these basic steps will be helpful.

About This Book

This book contains a wealth of marketing tips and suggestions, but not all family child care providers have the same need for these ideas. If you are just starting out, you may need to fill four to six openings, whereas if you have been in business awhile you probably only need to fill one or two openings at a time. Do not attempt to try all of the marketing ideas in this book. If you are looking to fill one opening, start small. See page 112 for 10 low-cost marketing tips. It is not necessary to make extraordinary efforts at marketing. Many providers gain new clients based strictly on word-of-mouth from their current clients. Such providers should focus on marketing to current clients (see chapter 4). Other providers may need to spend much more time and money on marketing and will want to use more of the ideas in this book. Many of the marketing ideas presented here may be best carried out by family child care associations and other support networks. You may want to present some of these ideas to your group for them to implement on behalf of its members. This book is meant to be used selectively over a long period of time.

This book can help you if you are just starting out or if you have many years of experience. It discusses how to market to prospective clients (chapter 3) and current clients (chapter 4). It includes many ideas about how to promote your program if you have little money (chapter 5) or if you have a lot of money (chapter 6). It identifies the key organizations to approach that can help you market (chapter 7). It has a lengthy discussion of how to set your rates (chapter 8). It also offers some answers to questions about how to compete against a fancy new child care center and against unregulated providers (chapter 9). Finally, the Appendix contains samples of forms and checklists you can use as part of your marketing program.

Not every idea in this book will appeal to every provider. We encourage providers to think carefully about how much marketing is necessary for their business. We do not encourage providers to adopt dozens of new marketing tips at the expense of spending less time caring for children. Not every idea will work in your community. Sometimes the same marketing idea that failed this year will succeed next year. This book does not offer an in-depth marketing plan for your business. It is meant to be a practical guide that gives you the tools you need to develop your own marketing plan. Marketing involves not so much science as common sense that everyone can apply. The lists of ideas in this book may seem overwhelming to some, at first glance. We do not expect you to follow every idea presented in this book, but we hope you will be open to trying something new. After trying out several ideas, be sure to evaluate their impact (chapter 10) so that you can refocus your next marketing plan. To help you sort through all of the ideas in this book we have included an Annual Marketing Calendar in the Appendix, which can help you plan your marketing program throughout the year.

Throughout this book we often use the words *customer* and *client* to describe the parents who use your services. We know that some providers are uncomfortable using these words in their business. We believe that, for purposes of this guide, using these words helps to keep the focus on parent needs. We are not suggesting that all providers must market their program in the same way. Far from it! It is up to you to run your business however you want. We believe that all providers can do a better job by following the suggestions in this book that make the most sense to them. The time to start marketing your program is now. You may find out that it can also be fun!

Tax Tip

The costs of all the marketing ideas listed in this book are tax-deductible expenses for your business. This includes the cost to

- Mail your newsletter.
- Take pictures of the children in your care.
- Purchase business cards.
- Buy an answering machine.
- Buy this book!
- And much more.

This book identifies over 100 business expenses. Keep the receipt for any item you buy to help you market your business. Such business marketing expenses should be entered on your IRS Form Schedule C (Profit or Loss From Your Business), under the Advertising Expense line. This is the same whether you are regulated or exempt from regulations.

For more information about what's deductible as a business expense, see *The Basic Guide to Family Child Care Record Keeping* by Tom Copeland, published by Redleaf Press, 800-423-8309.

CHAPTER TWO

Promoting the Benefits of Your Program

Why should I enroll my child in your program? What does your program offer that other programs don't? Your ability to answer these questions will largely determine how successful you will be at marketing your business. You may believe that you run a wonderful program, but unless parents also think so, you won't succeed. The way to answer these two questions is to learn to immediately and consistently communicate the benefits that your program offers to parents.

Many providers do a poor job of communicating the benefits of their programs. When asked to describe her services, a provider might respond, "I'm a licensed provider, open from 6 A.M. to 6 P.M. Monday through Friday. I have a preschool opening and I am on the Food Program." This answer gives parents few reasons to want to enroll their child. The provider has merely listed the features of the program, not the benefits. A feature describes what the provider offers. A benefit tells parents how the children and parents will have their needs met. A feature focuses on the provider; a benefit focuses on the client.

Let's look again at the program description above and see the difference between a feature and a benefit:

Feature	Benefit
"I am licensed."	"My program meets a variety of health and safety standards that help ensure your child will be safe."
"I'm open from 6 A.M. to 6 P.M. Monday–Friday."	"I have convenient hours for a parent's work schedule."
"I'm on the Food Program."	"I serve nutritious meals that meet federal quality standards to help your child grow." (See pages 86–87 for more information about the Food Program.)

Providers should take the time to understand the difference between a feature and a benefit. This is not an easy concept to master. One way of thinking about this is to look at what you've previously written about your program (in a classified ad, flyer, or parent handbook) and ask the question "Why does it matter to the parent or the child?" If your description doesn't clearly address the needs of your clients, then it's probably a list of features, not benefits. Look again at the chart above. Why does it matter if the provider is licensed? Licensing is a measure that the provider has met certain health and safety standards. Parents care about health and safety, so providers should use these words when describing their program. The other key words in the benefits listed above are "convenient hours" and "nutritious meals." These are the things that parents care about.

Your goal should be to identify three or four key benefits of your program. You should memorize them so that you can repeat them at a moment's notice: when parents call, at a **parent interview**, or whenever you meet someone who asks you about your program. Post these key benefits next to your telephone, list them in your **business flyer**, include them in your newspaper advertising, publish them in your **newsletter**, and include them in your **enrollment packet.** Your benefits are the answer to the two questions posed at the beginning of this section.

How can you identify the benefits of your program? Many providers struggle trying to come up with examples. Here are some suggestions:

➤ When parents remove their child from your care, give them a parent evaluation form and review what they say they liked about your program. They will probably use the language of benefits.

➤ Ask your current clients what they like best about the care you provide.

➤ Ask other providers or friends to give you feedback about your program.

➤ Ask your licensor (or regulator) what she feels is unique about your program. If the regulator has asked parents to evaluate providers, ask to see what the evaluations said.

➤ Survey parents who have used your program in past years. Ask what they remember most about your program.

➤ Ask the children in your care what they like best about being in your care.

Try to come up with about 10 initial benefits. Weed out the benefits that most other providers could also claim. If you have benefits that are special or unique, emphasize them. You may want to list 10 benefits on a survey form and ask parents to choose the three that best describe your program. You also could ask for this information when you review your contract and policies.

Examples of Benefits

All providers have benefits that they can market to parents. Here are examples of how you might describe your benefits:

➤ You have years of experience in caring for children: "I have seen many childhood illnesses, so I can help you quickly assess your child's health. I also have a lot of experience in meeting the emotional needs of children as they grow up."

➤ You have no experience in caring for children: "I have a lot of energy and I am really excited about working with families. I have lots of ideas about how to help children, and I believe in listening closely to what parents want for their children. My home is clean and my toys are all new."

➤ You have a highly structured program: "Children need the structure of a schedule. They become more comfortable and confident and experience a stronger sense of control when they can predict what comes next."

➤ You have little structure in your program: "I believe that young children learn through playing. I encourage children to explore many different activities at their own speed. I help children develop their curiosity and creativity, which are valuable skills that will help them throughout their lives."

If you are a little bashful about describing your benefits to parents, here is a suggestion: Collect information from your current and past clients about your benefits. When you talk to a prospective client, say, "This is what other parents who have used my services said they liked about my program." Then describe the benefits other parents have mentioned to you. Some providers may find it easier to express themselves using this technique.

Our society is becoming more and more a diverse blending of races, religions, cultures, ethnic backgrounds, and classes. It is important for all providers to understand the importance of this diversity when they market their program. Providers should learn more about their potential clients, take the time to make sure their program is responsive to the needs of all their current and potential clients, and be assertive in marketing their attention to diversity as a benefit of their program.

In defining your benefits you should emphasize the positive aspects of what you do. It is not necessary to criticize other programs and how they operate.
There are many different ways to deliver high-quality child care. Here are its basic ingredients:

- Children are in a small group: This ensures proper supervision and individualized care.
- The caregiver is reliable: This helps build a strong and stable relationship between the child and an adult.
- The caregiver is responsive to the emotional and developmental needs of children: This enables children to learn and grow at their own pace.
- There is effective communication between the caregiver and the parent: This helps ensure that the child is receiving consistent messages.
- The child's environment is healthy and safe: This will protect the child from hazardous conditions.
- The child's environment provides stimulation for learning: This will offer enough space for exercise and will expose the child to new ideas.

The fundamental outcome of high-quality child care is that young children will learn so that they can succeed in school and in life. Your benefits should help you communicate the message to parents that your primary concern is to help children meet this goal. Parents want their children to learn, but they don't always associate learning with family child care. You should use words such as "learning" and "teaching" a lot with parents. You are, after all, the children's first teacher, after their parents. How can you help educate parents about what learning looks like in family child care? Here are some things you can point to:

- Children setting the table: They are learning about counting, cooperation with others, and developing coordination by picking up and placing small objects.
- Dance: They are learning to understand simple movement directions and how to coordinate their entire body.

- Story time: They are learning to listen and retain information with their eyes and ears. They recognize words and pictures.

For more examples, see Skills Children Learn in Family Child Care in the Appendix.

When developing your list of benefits, don't use complicated words or jargon. Benefits should be stated using clean, understandable language. Instead of saying, "We use developmentally appropriate toys," say, "We give children toys that are challenging and fun for their age."

Here are some examples of benefits that providers might use to describe their program:

- Accredited by the National Association for Family Child Care (NAFCC)
- Affordable rates*
- Available for all ages of children, including infants, so parents don't have to separate siblings
- Care for mildly ill children so parents won't have to miss work
- Child Development Associate (CDA) credential or an advanced degree in early childhood education
- Child-led curriculum with planned learning activities and weekly themes led by an experienced preschool teacher
- Close interaction with parents, supportive of families
- Close to a state park/public swimming pool/playground
- Close to the client's home
- Computer learning games available
- Computer programs available for children 18 months and older
- Enclosed yard for safe, fun outdoor activities
- Energetic mother who loves children
- Enrichment program in foreign language or another culture
- Etiquette instruction that teaches manners
- Flexible hours to meet a parent's busy schedule
- Former dance instructor/nurse/singer/actor/musician
- Grandmother who has raised 11 of her own children
- Home-cooked, nutritious meals served
- Home environment where children feel safe and comfortable
- Individual care and attention in a home-based program

*There is a perception among many parents that family child care is less expensive than child care centers. Many providers do currently charge less than centers, but some currently charge more. Although there are good reasons for why some providers in a highly competitive area may want to market themselves as less expensive than the competition, in general, it is not a good idea for providers to compete on this basis. If more providers start competing with lower prices, this will contribute to driving down the rates for everyone. It will lower the average rates charged in a community, which will reduce the amount providers receive in government subsidies for low-income parents. We want to create a new impression among parents that family child care is a place where high-quality care can be found, not a place to find lower rates.

- Informal, non-institutional family care
- Instruction in religion or nonreligious moral ethics that teaches moral values
- Male caregiver to help children from female-headed families bond with a male adult
- Minimum television viewing
- Mixed-age grouping (and sibling care) so children can help teach other children and learn from those older than they are
- Multicultural program educates children about different cultures
- Open 24 hours a day to provide flexible hours to meet the needs of parents
- Piano lessons
- Planned activities geared to each child's interests
- Planned events with other providers to increase opportunities for children to socialize with others of their own age
- Regular field trips in the community (nature walks, local businesses) so children are exposed to new places
- Small group size so your child will receive more individual attention
- Specialty in infant/toddler/school-age care
- Stable, dependable provider with 10 years of experience
- Variety of stimulating toys and learning activities that are rotated throughout the year so children won't get bored

You Can Compete with Any Program

No program can offer everything for every child's needs. You should not be discouraged if you see other programs that offer features you don't have. You also offer benefits someone else does not have. You might be closer to a park, have more experience with infants, or offer longer hours. Your program can also compete with any child care center. Below is the list of benefits of a major child care center chain, taken directly from its national Web site. Read these benefits and think about how your program compares:

Age-appropriate curriculum designed by a Ph.D.

High standards of safety and security

Flexible hours 6:30 A.M.–6 P.M.

Specially trained teachers

Hot meals and two snacks served daily

Safe transportation

Open door policy for parents

State-of-the-art facilities

You probably now offer many of these benefits: high standards of safety, flexible hours, hot meals and two snacks, safe transportation, and an open-door policy. You may have some training credentials that compare well against a child care center teacher, and your home might have a security system. What's the benefit of a "state-of-the-art facility"? It's not clear. If you have well-designed play areas for children with child-size furniture and plenty of toys and other stimulating activities, then your home is also state-of-the-art. Many early childhood care and education experts say that a home environment is usually better for children than a commercial institution. What about the curriculum designed by a Ph.D.? Can you compete here? You may be using a curriculum program such as Mother Goose, Home Preschool, Everyday TLC, Red Umbrella, or others that are suitable for use in family child care. You may be using a "child-led" format that is an excellent way to organize learning experiences for young children. You may also be relying on your experiential knowledge gained through putting child development theory into daily practice for many years. Your program may also have a variety of other benefits that this chain does not. For example, you may offer an enrichment program in a foreign language. For more information about how to compete with centers, see pages 105–106.

Identifying and communicating the benefits of your program to parents is the cornerstone of your marketing efforts. Providers should feel confident that their benefits will attract parents to their programs.

CHAPTER THREE

Marketing to Prospective Clients

You want to make a good first impression when a parent contacts you. The three most important contact times with prospective clients are
- When they first see your home
- When they first call you on the phone
- When they come to your home for an interview

In your first contacts with parents you want to be able to identify their needs, communicate your program's benefits quickly, and make the parents feel comfortable. Show the parents that you are providing a solution to their problem. This requires skill in handling people as well as skill in using written materials to explain your program. This chapter describes how you can accomplish both.

Be sure to keep track of how parents learned about your program. Measure the effectiveness of your promotional activities (**keepsakes, business flyer, local parade**, word of mouth) by using the Parent Call Tracking Form in the Appendix.

Appearance of Your Home

First impressions are important to your business. Make sure the parents have a positive impression of what they first see on the outside and inside of your home. You should prepare your home as if you were selling it (which in a way, you are). Walk around the front of your home and into the entryway. Do you think parents would want to leave their children here? Below are some tips to present a clean, safe, and inviting appearance for your home:

➤ Make sure your home's street number is clearly visible from the road so parents can find you easily.
➤ Mow your lawn and pull weeds regularly.
➤ Keep your house freshly painted, screens in good repair, and brickwork mortared.
➤ Keep your dog behind a secure fence.

➤ Plant flowers in the front yard or display flower boxes in the windows or on the porch.

➤ Clean the front windows often.

➤ Put away yard tools and garden hose.

➤ Store leaves in decorative garbage bags.

➤ Take in the newspapers and mail right away.

➤ If your car is parked out front, keep it clean inside and out.

➤ Look at the back of your house and your alley. Clean things up, including any overflowing garbage cans.

➤ If you have a **business sign** in your front yard, make sure it is in good shape.

Examine the entryway of your home. Parents should feel welcome, comfortable, and safe as they first walk into your home. Here are some touches to add to create a welcome feeling:

➤ Have some items (children's drawings or photographs) posted at a child's level to make the child feel welcome.

➤ Make the entryway the cleanest area of your home. Put away all clutter. Although your play areas are likely to be filled with toys, it is better to keep the entryway clean.

➤ Eliminate bad odors from cooking, dirty diapers, or pets by using an unscented odor neutralizer (some people are allergic to fragrance sprays).

➤ Post photos of children, your credentials, and a schedule of activities on a nearby **bulletin board.** Take down notices reminding parents to pay you.

➤ Turn down any loud TV or music.

➤ Keep pets penned up.

➤ Have your **enrollment packet** readily available.

After you have completed this checklist, ask a friend with young children to come over and tour the outside and entryway of your home and give you feedback. An objective point of view can give you a fresh perspective.

How to Be a Good Neighbor

Before starting your child care business it is strongly advised that you check your local zoning ordinances, homeowner's association bylaws, or rental agreement to make sure you are not prohibited from operating. The Child Care Law Center has some excellent publications on zoning restrictions and family child care providers (see the Appendix). Assuming you are entitled to run a business from your home, you should announce to the neighbors on your block that you are about to begin caring for children in your home. You can do this by dropping off your **business flyer** or a **door**

hanger at their front door. A better way is to stop by and talk with each neighbor individually. You want to listen to any neighbor concerns and head off complaints before they become serious. Neighbors who are rude to your families or complain to child care regulators can create problems.

Neighbors may be unhappy about having a child care program opening nearby for several reasons: noise, parking, safety, property values, and appearance of your yard. If you are open to talking about these issues with your neighbors, they shouldn't be permanent obstacles. First, tell your neighbors about your plans for your business. Be especially clear about the maximum number of children you will care for and the hours you will be open. Some neighbors may imagine that you will have 30 children in your home. Reassure them that there will be many fewer children than this in your home at any one time. Because of the small numbers involved, noise is usually not a problem. Remind neighbors that you will be home every day and can keep a protective eye on the neighborhood. If you will be offering second-shift or overnight care, prepare a brief list of rules for your families to follow (for example, no car-door slamming or horn honking to announce a parent's arrival), and share this with your neighbors. Ask what else you can do to keep noise down.

Parking concerns are often not a problem in family child care. Inform neighbors that there will only be a few cars stopping by twice a day. If you care for more than one child in a family, point out that even fewer cars will drive by. If there is limited space, ask parents to stagger their drop-off and pickup times if possible. Ask parents never to block or use a neighbor's driveway. Safety concerns can be addressed by telling neighbors that you have liability insurance, that you will strictly follow all child care regulations, and that you will use your common sense. Ask for any specific safety questions from neighbors so you can respond with a plan to address them. There is little evidence that property values are affected by family child care. Ask your local property tax office or real estate agent for information on this. If you are concerned that local laws may restrict the operation of family child care, have a friend call the local property tax office under the pretext of doing research, and have the information mailed to your friend's address. The best you may be able to do is to try to reassure neighbors that you also have an interest in keeping property values up and that some families are more likely to want to live in a neighborhood with a nearby child care provider. Nobody wants to live next to someone with a messy, unkempt yard. Keep your play area tidy every day. You may want to put up a privacy fence to block off your backyard.

If you keep talking to neighbors about what your business is doing, you shouldn't have many problems. Be aware, though, that by being public about your program, you may run into some opposition from neighbors who otherwise might not have known you were operating a business near them. If you are concerned about this, you may not want to be so public with neighbors about your business. In most cases, however, neighbors are happy to have a provider close by. Invite your neighbors to an open house when you are getting started. Distribute your **business cards** and **flyers** and tell them what openings you have. Throw an Easter egg hunt, **Halloween** party, Labor Day picnic, "good neighbor day party," or holiday party for the children and your neighbors in the community. Ask neighbors to talk to you first if they have any questions or concerns about what you are doing. Happy neighbors can help you market your program through positive word of mouth.

A special problem can exist for providers who rent or live in a housing development run by a homeowner's association. Local and state laws govern the rights of renters or homeowners in these situations. In many areas landlords or housing covenants can prohibit the operation of any business, including family child care. For legal help, contact the Child Care Law Center (see the Appendix). Before opening your business, you should check to see if there are any restrictions on running a business out of your home. If you face opposition, use the arguments described in this chapter. Try to point out that your particular business doesn't really create any serious problems for others. Ask your **family child care association** to help you lobby for changes in restrictive laws affecting providers.

Recorded Telephone Greeting

When a parent calls you at your place of business and you can't answer the phone, you don't want to lose the call. If your phone rings and rings and there is no answering machine to record a message, current clients will worry and prospective clients will call

Hello! You have reached April's Playhouse and the Beckman residence. No one can come to the phone right now because we are busy with the children Please leave a message & we will call you back as soon as we can Thank you very much for calling!

another provider. Therefore, it is imperative that you have an answering machine or voice mail (which is available through many local phone companies) with a recorded greeting from you on it that asks parents to leave a message. You want your recorded greeting to leave a positive, professional impression on the caller. A greeting that has the noise of crying children in the background, or a garbled message, will alienate the caller. Instead, leave a greeting that indicates that you can't answer the phone because you are with the children. This statement of priority will impress most parents. Here are some additional suggestions:

➤ Your greeting should identify the name of your business. For example, "Hello! You have reached April's Playhouse and the Beckman residence. This is April Beckman. No one can come to the phone right now because we are busy with the children. Please leave a message and we will call you back as soon as we can. Thank you very much for calling."

➤ If you want to keep your business and personal messages separate, consider purchasing a telephone service that allows you to record messages in two different places. Your greeting might now say, "Hello! You have reached April's Playhouse and the Beckman residence. This is April Beckman. If you would like to leave a message for April's Playhouse, press one now. If you would like to leave a message for April, Bill, Sylvia, or Brian, press two now." Record the rest of your business greeting after the parent presses one.

➤ Some providers purchase a second phone line that they use for all business calls. Although the cost of the first phone line into your home is not tax deductible, the business portion of a second line is deductible.

➤ Your own child or the children in your care may deliver the greeting as long as they speak clearly and the message is short. Be sure to get the permission of parents before you use their child's voice. (See the Photo, Voice, and Video Permission Form in the Appendix.)

➤ Don't use a commercial greeting service that uses impersonators of famous people. Don't use an exotic or silly greeting. These are not professional or reassuring, and they may offend some people.

➤ Make sure parent callers can leave a long message. Don't use an answering machine or voice mail that cuts off after only one minute.

➤ You want your greeting to start playing after no more than three unanswered rings. Don't make parents wait and wait before they can leave a message.

➤ Get a cordless phone to carry with you in the backyard or cell phone to carry with you on field trips, to reduce the number of unanswered calls. Some providers also have car phones and pagers. Note: The business portion of such telephone equipment is deductible.

➤ After recording your greeting, ask a friend to call your number, listen to the message, and give you constructive feedback. You want to sound clear, positive, and energetic.

➤ You may want to tell parents that if they call you during the day they will probably get your answering machine. Reassure them that you check often for messages and that you will return their calls promptly. Establish times when you will be easier to reach, so parents know the best time to call.

➤ Because you are in the business of caring for children, try to keep all phone calls short during business hours so you don't take your attention away from the children.

➤ Finally, in some parts of the country telephone companies may treat providers as commercial customers and charge them a higher commercial rate on their monthly phone bill. Despite this, it is still worthwhile to record a business greeting.

How to Handle Phone Calls from Prospective Clients

Every phone call from a prospective client has the potential to result in new business. It is your chance to make a good first impression. How you handle each call is therefore very important. Some parents may sound very organized over the phone and have a list of specific questions. Other parents may not be sure what to ask you. What every parent wants to know is, "Will this program meet the needs of my child and my family?" and "Is there something special about this program that will make a difference in my decision of where to enroll my child?" Because of this, you need to be an active, rather than a passive, communicator on the phone. This means you should take charge of the phone conversation by asking questions of the parent, rather than just responding to what the parent asks you. You should be the first one to decide whether or not you want the parent to come over for an interview. Take the attitude that you are choosing the parent, not that you are waiting for the parent to choose you. Follow this three-step process for every parent phone call:

1) Find out the specific needs of the parent and the child.
2) Briefly describe the benefits of your program.
3) Get the parent to agree to come over to your house for an interview.

Step one is to find out the specific needs of the parent and the child. Your goal here is to quickly assess whether or not your program can meet these needs. If not, you don't want to spend any more time than necessary to politely tell the parent that your program isn't a good fit for those needs.

Start by asking questions about the child, such as
- How old is your child?
- What are your child's needs?
- What hours do you need care?
- What does your child enjoy doing?
- What are you looking for in a program for your child?

By asking such questions, you can help the parent relax while you listen for any major issues that would tell you that your program is not a good fit for what the parent wants. If you think things won't work out, don't hesitate to decide against enrolling the child. In this case, tell the parent, "I don't think my program can meet the needs of your child as you have described them. I think you should look for another caregiver. Thanks for calling." You may want to offer to refer this parent to another provider or to your local **Child Care Resource and Referral agency.**

The second step, if the parent sounds promising, is to briefly describe the key benefits of your program: "I offer a structured program that prepares children to enter their school years eager to learn. We have a large backyard where children can run and play and have a lot of fun." If you have posted the top three benefits of your program by your phone, now is the time to share these with the parent. Try to relate your program's benefits to the needs previously expressed by the parent. In other words, if the parent talked about how his child enjoys learning about nature, you might describe your regular field trips to a nearby park. Don't be afraid to express how proud you are of what you do.

There is no one way to handle a phone interview. Some providers prefer to say as little as possible about their program over the phone. Once they have decided that they can meet the parent's needs, their only goal is to get the parent to come over for an interview. They believe that the way to market their business is in person. The more they describe their services over the phone, the easier they believe it is to turn a prospective client off. For example, a parent might think the provider is too far away, but after coming over and seeing the program she is willing to make the trip. Or, a parent wants to spend $120 tops, but after meeting the provider is willing to pay $135. A provider might have a terrific curriculum but can't show this over the phone. When a parent calls, he might be looking for an answer to one particular question that is so important that if the provider gives the wrong answer, the parent may not want to come over for an interview. To avoid this problem some providers simply don't discuss the details of their programs on the phone. Instead they convey to the parent, "You have to see my program before you can make a decision."

Step three is to get the parent to agree to come to your home for an interview. This is the ultimate goal of every phone call. Invite parents by asking a question that they can't say "no" to. For example, say, "Would you like to come to visit next Tuesday or Wednesday?" Don't ask, "Would you like to make an appointment for an interview?" If the parent can't decide whether or not to schedule an interview, tell the parent you'll call back in a day or two after he has had time to think about it. It is important to schedule the interview as soon as possible (within three or four days) because parents may have already scheduled interviews with other providers. Here are some tips for handling parent phone calls.

➤ Place the phone where loud noise from your child care children and other distractions are minimized. Perhaps you can explain to your children that you need to have quiet time when you are on the phone.

➤ Place the following items by each phone in your home so you are ready to handle phone calls.

- Pen or pencil
- Parent Call Tracking Form (See the Appendix.)
- A list of your top three program benefits

➤ Answer all phone calls with a business, not a personal, greeting. Foɪ example, "Hello, Juanita's Playhouse. This is Juanita. May I help you?" Don't answer the phone by saying, "Hello?" or "Yeah?" or "What?" or "Juanita's residence."

➤ At the very start of your conversation, ask for the parent's name, complete address, and phone number. Next, ask for the names and ages of the children she is seeking care for, and how she heard about your program. Use this opportunity to track the effectiveness of your promotions and advertising. If the parent mentions the name of someone who referred her to you, make a note of this name and send a thank-you note later. It is easier to remember to ask this information if you use your Parent Call Tracking Form. A sample is shown in the Appendix.

➤ As you are talking with the parent, try to always sound positive and maintain an upbeat tone of voice. Smile while you are speaking. You will sound friendlier. How you sound on the phone is as important as what you say. Don't scream at your children while you are on the phone. If you are too distracted, excuse yourself, deal quickly with the problem, and then come back to finish the call.

➤ If you are very busy or having a bad day, you may not want to answer the phone; in this situation, let your answering machine or voice mail record parent calls. Return calls when it is more convenient and you are more in control. If you do answer the phone when you are distracted, ask for the parent's name and phone number and tell him you will call back when it's more convenient for you. For example, "Thank you for calling. I'm in the middle of an activity with the children right now. May I call you back in a few minutes? I appreciate your understanding. At what number can I reach you?" Parents are more likely to be impressed that your first priority is the children rather than being upset that you can't talk right away. It's better not to talk with parents unless you can give them your full attention while feeling confident about yourself and your program. If you can't call back right away, give the parent a realistic time when you can return the call and then fulfill your promise.

➤ If others in your family answer the phone, discuss with them how you would like them to handle such calls. You want them to be courteous, friendly, and helpful. They might say, "Hello, this is the Wang residence and Yei's Child Care. This is Justin speaking. May I help you?… No, my mother can't come to the phone right now because she is with the children. May I take your name and number and have her call you back shortly?"

➤ After the phone call is over, send a thank-you note or postcard, even if it is obvious that the parent will not enroll in your program. If you have scheduled the parent for an interview, send a thank-you note along with a Choosing a Child Care Program Checklist (see the Appendix). In addition, mail your **business flyer** and a reminder notice a few days before the interview.

➤ A difficult parent question to answer on the phone is "How much do you charge?" Some providers will answer this question clearly and directly; others tell parents that they must come over for an interview before discussing rates. There is no simple answer for everyone. You don't want to lose a potential client based on your rates before you've had a chance to promote your program. On the other hand, you don't want to spend several hours in an interview only to have the parent decline to enroll their child because your rates seem too high. It is important not to be defensive in discussing rates. Explain that the value of your service comes from the benefits you offer. If a parent complains about your rates, give a reason for them. "My rates are based on my five years of experience as a provider, my CDA credentials, and the variety of special field trips we take each month." One way some providers handle this question is to tell parents they would be happy to mail them a copy of their rate schedule. Sending a written rate schedule is an authoritative and professional way to communicate. Other providers are very straightforward about discussing their rates on the phone. They want to weed out those parents who are simply price shopping. One provider tells callers, "I'm not the cheap alternative. If you are looking for the cheapest care, you should keep looking. I have a master's degree in early childhood education and seven years of experience in caring for young children, and I use a planned curriculum that promotes the learning and emotional development of the children. I would be happy to schedule an interview with you and your child. I have time next Monday or Tuesday evening. Which time would work best for you?" For a further discussion of rates, see chapter 8.

➤ Occasionally you may get a call from a parent who is in a hurry to enroll a child after talking with you for only a few minutes. How do you handle this? First, you should be hesitant to enroll any child without a face-to-face interview. Invite the parent and the child for an interview right away. If the parent refuses to come to an interview and insists that you agree to enroll the child right away, this is a bad sign, and you should probably not consent. If the parent needs care immediately, you may want to enroll the child on a drop-in basis and charge by the day for the first two weeks to see how it works out. Make it clear that your daily rate will cost more per week than your normal weekly rate (see chapter 8).

➤ If you are getting parent calls but find that very few of the parents are accepting your invitation for an interview, this is a sign to reevaluate what you are doing. Conduct a self-examination to determine what you might be saying on the phone or how you are saying it that is causing parents to turn you down. Go over several recent phone conversations with a friend and ask for suggestions on what you might be able to do differently. Ask a friend to do follow-up calls with parents to discover what they liked and disliked about your program. If you are easily able to get parents to come over for an interview but none of them are acceptable to you, try to think of ways you can more carefully screen parents on the phone so you don't waste so much time with interviews.

Talking about Special Needs

Under the Americans with Disabilities Act (ADA), it is illegal to discriminate against a parent or a child who has a disability. What do you do if the parent tells you on the phone that the child has a disability such as asthma, epilepsy, Attention Deficit Disorder, or AIDS? Here are some tips:

➤ You are required to do what a reasonable person would do to provide appropriate care for the child. You are not required to provide care if doing so would cause you significant difficulty or significant expense or would fundamentally alter the nature of your program. Therefore, you cannot say, "I don't provide care for children with disabilities," or "I don't provide care for children who use a wheelchair." You must consider the needs of each child and explore how you could offer appropriate care. You cannot charge more to care for children with special needs. There is an excellent publication that describes how the ADA law applies to family child care. It is called "Caring for Children with Special Needs: The ADA Act and Child Care" and is published by the Child Care Law Center. (See the Appendix.) The Center also publishes other booklets on the ADA and child care.   .

➤ Do not decline to conduct an interview with a parent simply because the child has a disability. If you do so, you could be in violation of the ADA law.

➤ Ask the parent on the phone and at the interview what kind of accommodations, if any, the child may need to be a part of your program. If you are not sure how you can provide appropriate care for the child, ask questions. Seek help from outside resources such as a public health nurse, your regulatory worker, or your **Child Care Resource and Referral agency.**

➤ You should see caring for children with special needs as a business opportunity. Parents are looking for someone to care for their child; they are not looking to sue you. Many providers have been caring for children who have a variety of disabilities for many years without problems. There are a growing number of children with special needs who will need child care in the future. The more experience you have with caring for such children, the more you can successfully market yourself to this audience.

How to Handle Interviews with Parents

The parent interview is probably your most important opportunity to market your business. Make sure you are doing everything you can to make a good impression. There are three goals you should pursue at a parent interview:

1) Determine if the parent's and child's needs are a good match for your program.
2) Explain the benefits of your program.
3) Ask the parent to enroll in your program.

The parent interview process can be handled in many different ways. There is no one way that works best for every parent or provider.

Should you conduct a parent interview in the evening or during your business hours? Should the child be present at the interview? Should both parents (if there are two) be present? Not all providers answer these questions in the same way. The benefit of an evening interview is that it is usually more convenient for parents and allows time for discussion without distractions. The disadvantage is that parents can't see your program in action. If the child is present you can more easily evaluate if he or she will be a good match with the other children. In a two-parent family it is crucial for both parents to attend the parent interviews. If one parent doesn't have time to participate in this important discussion, then it is likely that you cannot count on this parent later to help deal with behavioral or financial problems.

Providers handle parent interviews in a variety of ways. Some conduct only one interview with parents. Others conduct their parent interview in two stages. First, the provider meets in the evening with just the parents, answers questions, and gives a tour of the home. If both parties are still interested, a second meeting is scheduled with the parent and child during business hours to see if the child will fit in. There are even a few providers who visit the parent's home for a final interview to get a better idea of the child's home environment and to learn more about how the child interacts with his parents. Here are some tips to consider for your parent interview:

➤ Call the parent a few days before the interview to confirm the appointment. If you have already sent a postcard reminder, you may not want to call. If you do, say that you look forward to his visit. If the parent wants to cancel the interview, thank him for his interest. Ask him to reconsider your program at a future time.

➤ In preparation for the interview make sure your house looks orderly. Make the beds and do the dishes. You want your home to look like a place that is friendly to children, so don't put away all the toys and over-clean. Dress comfortably.

➤ Set up a quiet area of your home where you can sit down and have an extended conversation with parents. Ask family members not to disturb you during the interview. If the interview is conducted during your business hours, have a helper or family member take charge of the children at this time.

➤ Spend a little time talking and playing with the parent's child, but don't come on too strong. Tell the parent, "If I seem to be ignoring your child it's because I like to let children come to me instead of pouncing on them." At the end of the interview you might want to give the child a small present (possibly a **keepsake**) and a certificate to celebrate her official "visit" to your program.

➤ You should have an open mind at the start of each interview. Make it clear to the parent at the beginning that both the parent and you have to agree to enroll a child. Sometimes parents think that it's just up to them. Don't hesitate to turn a parent down if you believe that conflicts with the parent or the child would be too hard for you to handle.

➤ Rather than spending a lot of time describing your program to begin with, you may want to have the parent start off by asking questions. Listen carefully to the parent's needs and concerns. Take notes if this will help you remember more easily. See the Parent Interview Checklist in the Appendix. Keep a copy of your checklist for your files. (If you put the parent on your waiting list, refer to this checklist again before enrolling the child.) Respond to the specific issues raised by a parent. Parents who have their questions answered first are more likely to feel at ease and be more receptive to you and your program.

➤ Ask open-ended questions to help you identify parent and child needs. An open-ended question is one that cannot be answered with a simple yes or no. Examples: "What would be the most important thing I could do to help your child grow?" "What are your child's special interests?" "What do you see your child doing in three months, one year, five years?" This last question can help you identify parents' expectations for their child. Your response should be to point out how your program can meet these expectations.

➤ Present the parents with a package of written materials about your program. Arrange these materials in a colorful folder with, possibly, your business name on the front. Have one package available for each parent. Your package might include the following:
   • Business card **for both parents**
   • Business flyer
   • Choosing Child Care Checklist
   • A description of your philosophy of child caring
   • References from current or previous clients

- Background credentials: years of experience, training credentials, and educational degrees
- Your contract and policies describing your rates, payment policies, hours, daily schedule, paid vacations, and holidays
- An **enrollment form** for parents to sign
- Sample menus from the Food Program

➤ Give a tour of your business. As you walk through the inside and outside of your home, emphasize that it is a safe, fun, and creative place to learn. What may be obvious to you may not be so for some parents. Tell them what they are seeing. Here are examples of what you might say:

"All the electrical outlets are covered to protect the children."

"I always make sure that dangerous household chemicals and objects are locked behind these cupboards or doors to keep your children safe."

"We have child-sized furniture and pillows so the children can feel comfortable and safe."

"We have a variety of toys and books available to the children. We rotate toys from storage every few months so the children don't get bored."

"The floors in this room are carpeted and there are no sharp edges on the furniture to avoid injury to the children if they fall."

"We keep the curtains open to create a light and cheerful atmosphere that the children enjoy."

"We serve nutritious meals, including breakfast, a morning snack, lunch, and an afternoon snack."

"I rock babies on this rocking chair every day."

"Here is where I read to the children every day in the afternoon."

"Our outdoor equipment is constantly used by the children. It helps them to exercise and have fun."

➤ If you have prepared a **scrapbook** or **photo album** that illustrates different aspects of your program, show it to the parents and their children.

➤ After you have finished the tour of your home and you've answered all the parent's questions, it is time to make a decision. If you want to enroll the child, ask the parent, "Are you ready to make a decision to enroll your child at this time or do you need a few days to think about it? If you can decide today I have the paperwork here for you to fill out." If the parent is not ready to make a decision, ask, "Is there anything else I can do to help you make a decision today?" If the parent needs more time, say, "When do you think you will be able to make a decision? Can I call you at that time?" It is a good idea to give the parent a specific deadline to make a decision. If you have other prospective parents who are interested in your program, you should tell the parent this. If the parent does not call you by the deadline, call her to confirm that she is not interested. Setting a deadline allows you to quickly fill your opening rather than being kept waiting by a parent.

➤ If you decide you do not want to enroll the child, tell the parent, "I don't think this would be a good fit for your child at this time. It's nothing personal about you or your child. My decision is based on my own feelings." Don't elaborate on your reasons. Don't criticize or blame the parent or the child. The parent will never agree with your reasons and will probably be upset if you explain yourself. Remind the parent that earlier you explained that both of you had to agree before the child could be enrolled. If possible, you want the parent to leave without feeling negative about your program, to reduce the chances of her speaking ill of your program to others.

➤ If you are conducting a lot of interviews but having few parents want to enroll in your program, this may be a sign that you need to reevaluate what you are doing. Examine closely what might be going wrong. Was your home presentable? Did the parents show signs of disapproval of things you said or about your policies? You may want to ask a friend to call the parents and conduct a quick survey. The questions to ask might be

"Have you found care for your child? If so, why did you choose that program?"

"What did you like about my program?"

"What did you dislike about my program?"

"What could have been different about this program that would have changed your mind?"

Review the answers to these questions with your friend and see if there is anything you could do differently for the next interview. For further advice, ask an experienced provider for assistance.

➤ If you are nervous about conducting interviews with parents, you may want to role-play the entire process with a friend. Ask the friend for honest feedback: Were you friendly, and did you put the parent at ease? Did you ask specific questions about the parent's needs? Did you clearly explain your program's benefits? Did you ask directly for the parent to enroll the child? Sometimes all it takes to conduct a good interview with parents is practice.

When to Say No to Enrolling a Child

It may seem strange to say this in a book about marketing your program and building enrollment, but there may be situations in which you should not enroll a child. Your goal as a business is to provide a quality service to parents and children. If your service doesn't fit well for a particular child or family, you will be doing everyone a favor by not signing a contract with that parent. If you enroll a child, knowing that there are potential problems, and end up terminating care later under a cloud of bad feelings, you, the parent, and the child will be dissatisfied. You want to avoid short-term relationships with families. To prevent bad word of mouth from such a situation, don't be afraid to say no before care begins.

What clues should you look for in determining a mismatch? There are no absolutes, but here are a few signs:

- The parent refuses to give you the name of a previous caregiver as a reference.
- The child seems out of control. (Note: Under the ADA, providers may not discriminate against children with disabilities. See page 26 for a further discussion about the ADA.)
- The parent does not seem interested in her own child or the kind of care you say you will be offering.
- The parent does not treat you with respect or does not show a willingness to be flexible about adapting to your program.
- The parent seems uncomfortable with your rates or payment policies.
- The parent wants you to make special accommodations for him or his child that you are uncomfortable making.

Clearly, not every provider will react the same way to every parent. It pays, however, to trust your feelings about the parent and child. Many providers offer a two-week trial period to help sort out any potential conflicts or mismatches. Either parent or provider may terminate during this trial period without giving any notice.

If you have made the decision to not enroll a child, how do you say no to the parent? You do not want to be negative or critical about either the child or the parent. Such criticism will only backfire on you when the parent talks to someone else about you. The best thing to say is, "I don't feel that this is the best place for your child at this time." Such a neutral statement does not place blame, and it allows the parent to back off gracefully. Do not elaborate or give further explanation for your decision. You are allowed to make many decisions in your business based on your personal feelings, and this is one more example. You may want to refer the parent to the local **Child Care Resource and Referral agency,** the **family child care association,** or the local **child care regulatory office** for help in finding another provider. Doing so may ease the mind of the parent after your refusal.

Follow-up Contacts

Sometimes a prospective client will make an initial call or visit your program and then fail to contact you again. There may be many reasons for this: the parent has called a number of providers and can't make up her mind; the parent decided not to change her current child care arrangement for now; or the parent has chosen another provider. With an increasing number of child care options to choose from, some parents have difficulty sorting out one provider from another. In order to help the parent remember you, follow-up is important. Here are some follow-up tips:

➤ Always ask for prospective parents' phone numbers and addresses when they first call.

➤ Ask the parents for permission to give them a follow-up call within a week.

➤ After they call or come over for an interview, send them a short thank-you note. Tell them you appreciate the time they spent with you.

➤ Mention a benefit of your program to remind parents why they should enroll with you: "As we discussed, I will be able to care for Irene as early as 6 A.M. on Wednesdays to accommodate your work schedule."

➤ Write all notes by hand. Your service is too personal to send a form letter. You may want to enclose a **keepsake** with your note.

If you don't hear back from the parent after sending the note, place a follow-up call. Ask the parent if he received your information. Ask if he has any questions. Ask if he is still looking for care. If not, ask what caused him to choose his new provider. Make notes of the reasons; this may help you with the next prospective parent who contacts you. If the parent says he chose another provider because that program offered more structured learning than yours, you may want to emphasize with the next parent the signs of how children learn under your program. You could say, "My children learn valuable skills of social interaction and self-control when I teach them how to put away their toys before taking a nap."

If the parent has not yet made a decision about child care when you call, ask if there is any further information you can provide. Offer another brief reminder about your program's benefits. "We are having a field trip to the zoo next month, which I am sure your child would enjoy." If you prepare **newsletters** for your current clients, send a copy of your last newsletter to this prospective parent with a final, brief note inviting the parent to contact you. No further follow-up is likely to be useful.

Many providers do not currently follow up, so if you start doing so, you are likely to make a positive, memorable impact on parents.

Child Care Flyer

When parents are looking for child care they may have a hard time knowing what questions to ask a provider. They may also need help in keeping track of all the programs they contacted. To help the parents remember your program, prepare a simple Choosing a Child Care Checklist flyer. See the Appendix for an example. You may want to use copies of flyers already developed by your local **Child Care Resource and Referral agency**, your local **family child care association**, or the National Association for Family Child Care. The National Association for the Education of Young Children has also developed a flyer for providers to use ("Choosing a Good Early Childhood Program" #525). See the Appendix for information on how to contact these organizations. If you use a flyer developed by someone else, put your name and phone number on it when you distribute it.

Send copies of your flyer to parents when they call or give them one when they come for an interview. Encourage parents to compare your program with others. Refer to the contents of the flyer to point out the benefits of your program. By doing so you are helping parents think of what they need to look for in choosing a child care program, and you are already providing a service that will make potential customers remember you.

Photo Album and Scrapbook

When parents come over to your home for an interview they will usually not spend enough time to see all of what your program has to offer. Assemble a photo album or scrapbook (both are cheaper than making a videotape) that you display on a table for parents and child to thumb through during the interview process when you get busy or are interrupted. You can refer to it as you describe your program. The children in your care may also enjoy looking at your photo album and scrapbook. They will like to reflect on past group activities and experiences and remember friends who have left. A photo album should contain pictures that illustrate the benefits of your program:

- Children reading, playing, sleeping, and eating
- Special events: holiday celebrations, birthdays, field trips, a visiting puppet show
- Activities during different seasons of the year: winter play, rainy-day activities, wading pool fun
- Unique aspects of your program: computer activities, overnight events, trips to a summer cabin
- Art projects and holiday decorations made by the children

Some providers put captions underneath the photos in their album. Captions can help to identify more directly the benefits of your program. For example:

"Clean-up after lunch means cooperation."

"Holiday party with current and past families"

"Field trip to local park"

"Learning to read/share/count/dance/sing"

See Skills Children Learn in Family Child Care in the Appendix for more information on identifying what children are learning. You may want to make copies of the skills list in the Appendix and give it to your parents. When you show children learning, you are communicating the value of your program to parents.

A scrapbook can contain photos as well as other information, such as

- Accreditation, training, and **educational credentials**
- Past **parent evaluations**/references
- Descriptions of special activities
- Newspaper stories about your program
- A copy of your license
- A copy of your **business flyer**
- Certificates and awards
- Special or important visitors to your program such as an elected official, licensing worker, or puppeteer (Have these visitors sign a guest list.)
- Thank-you notes and cards from current and past clients

Enrollment Packet

An enrollment packet is a compilation of forms and information for the parent who is about to enroll in your program. This is easier to put together than you might think. It's not important for this packet to look slick, just neat and organized. You may want to distribute your packet at the end of an interview or mail it to parents a week before the first day of care. Your packet may include

- Enrollment forms: contract (hours, rates), medical consent forms, medical information forms, and policies (discipline guidance, sick policy, meals, field trips)
- Description of your services and special program activities or events
- A copy of your license or registration (Some providers prefer not to pass this out for fear that it may be forged by another provider.)
- A summary of your hours and days closed (holidays, vacations, professional days)
- Several copies of your **business card**
- The latest copy of your **newsletter**
- A copy of your **business flyer**

- Your resume
- A description of your philosophy of child caring
- Newspaper articles or other information about your program
- A flyer describing the benefits of family child care (You can use those developed by the National Association for the Education of Young Children or your local **Child Care Resource and Referral agency** may have one you can use. See the Appendix for information on how to contact these organizations.)

Your enrollment packet can look professional without being expensive. Purchase folders with pockets for flyers and business cards. Don't give out an enrollment packet unless a parent is signing up; it's too expensive to give to everyone who calls. Send your business flyer to those who call, before an interview.

Improve Your Education Credentials

Providing high-quality child care for young children of different ages and needs takes skill. To get this skill requires training and experience. Studies indicate that training in the area of child development is more important than experience with children when measuring high-quality care. That's why providers should do everything they can to improve their education credentials. In an increasingly competitive market, parents will be looking for objective standards of quality to help them choose a child care program. Accomplishments in the field of education will be even more important to many parents in the future.

Although there is no single educational achievement that all providers should attain, here are some training programs to explore:

➤ The National Association for Family Child Care (NAFCC) offers an accreditation program designed to promote and recognize high-quality, professional family child care. It is called The Quality Standards for NAFCC Accreditation. The program requires training, a self-study process, and a home visit by an observer. For contact information about this program, see the NAFCC listing in the Other Resources section of the Appendix.

➤ The Council for Early Childhood Professional Recognition has developed the Child Development Associate (CDA) credential to improve the quality of child care. It is an individual credential acquired through a non–college degree course of study. A provider must complete 120 hours of training in a variety of areas through technical colleges, **Child Care Resource and Referral agencies,** and workshops sponsored by other organizations. For further information, see the CDA listing in the Other Resources section of the Appendix.

➤ Providers may want to obtain a post-secondary degree in child development, elementary education, early childhood education, or school-age care. Many colleges and universities offer two-year or four-year programs. Providers who have post-secondary degrees in other fields that are relevant to children, such as nursing, general education, or foreign languages, can use these qualifications to improve the quality of care they offer and should list them as a benefit when describing their program. The types of post-secondary degrees offered by colleges and universities vary greatly by state. Contact your local educational institution for information about the most appropriate course of study for you. Also check to see if your **government child care subsidy agency** reimburses at a higher rate if you earn a post-secondary degree.

➤ There is a growing trend of receiving education degrees on-line. If you have access to the Internet, you may want to explore this possibility. The National Association of Child Care Resource and Referral Agencies also offers classes on-line for family child care providers. See the Appendix for its listing.

➤ Some states have special training projects and credential programs available for family child care providers. Contact your local **Child Care Resource and Referral agency** for further information about what is available in your area.

➤ Because our society is a multicultural community and your potential customers may come from increasingly diverse backgrounds, you should attend workshops to learn about different cultures so that all of your customers will feel comfortable in your program and so that you will be better able to help all of your children learn. Get to know other providers from different cultures and ask them for advice.

➤ Providers should take advantage of as many local training opportunities as possible in early childhood development and early care and education. Many organizations offer such training: **Child Care Resource and Referral agencies, Child and Adult Care Food Program sponsors,** community colleges, **family child care associations,** and universities. Contact your local CCR&R agency for further information.

➤ Turn your life experiences into credentials. Although studies show that training is more important than experience in defining high-quality care, providers should not lose sight of the fact that experience can make a difference. A mother or grandmother who has raised her own children and grandchildren can certainly claim knowledge about what it takes to be a caregiver. Life experiences combined with additional training and certification can be a powerful way you can compete.

Providers should use their education and life experiences to help market their program. Display your **credentials** to prospective parents (on your **bulletin board** and in your **newsletter**) and keep current clients informed of all new training classes and workshops you attend. Use every opportunity to show parents how the knowledge and skills you have mastered help you do a better job of teaching their child.

Display Your Credentials

Parents are looking for signs of high quality in their child's provider and program. One measure of this quality is educational credentials and other accomplishments and achievements. Because regulations vary so much from state to state, parents have little guidance from objective sources about whether your program is high quality. Displaying your training credentials is an important way to communicate high quality. You should take every opportunity to inform parents about your credentials. Here are some examples:

- Child Development Associate degree (CDA) *
- National Association for Family Child Care (NAFCC) Accreditation Program *
- Degree in child development or other child care–related field from a college or university
- Certificate of training from a state or local quality-improvement project (such as the type of project developed by Dayton Hudson Foundation)
- Classes in child development from local educational institutions
- A degree in nursing, home economics, elementary education, or other fields that are relevant to the care of children
- Community awards
- Awards from local and state **family child care associations**
- Child care license or registration certificate
- Service as an officer or board member of a family child care association
- Attendance at state or national child care conferences such as NAFCC, Quality Care for Children, or National Association for the Education of Young Children
- Food Program member
- Certificate of attendance at workshop sponsored by Food Programs, **Child Care Resource and Referral agencies,** or **family child care associations**
- Parent of four children of your own, grandparent of two
- Stories about your program in local newspapers

Display notices of these achievements on your **bulletin board** for prospective parents to see. Put accreditation and degrees on your business cards and on your **business flyers.** Announce new accomplishments in your **newsletter.** Put copies of your credentials in your **photo album or scrapbook** and in your **enrollment packet.** Frame your important credentials and permanently display them on your wall.

Offer a Special Service

With the growing number of child care programs for parents to choose from, it will become increasingly difficult to get parents to notice you. One way to stand out from

* See the Appendix for further information about these programs.

the competition is to offer a unique service for parents and their children. Below are some suggestions of special services you might offer. Think of any particular skill or interest you might have that could translate into a new service.

- Offer a special summer activity program involving extended field trips, ball games, swimming, camping, boating, gardening, or community art projects.
- Contact your local 4-H club to see if there is a way your program can collaborate with its activities.
- Plant a community garden in your backyard that involves your clients and their children. Use the garden to teach the children about plants and nutrition. Give them vegetables and spices to take home.
- Offer overnight care for special days (Valentine's Day, Mother's Day) or when parents go out to a play, to the opera, or bowling.
- Cook an occasional evening meal-to-go that parents order in advance to take home when they pick up their children.
- Bring in a gymnastics or ballet instructor to teach the children so that parents reduce the time they spend driving to these lessons.
- Provide haircuts for children.
- Offer music lessons.
- Take children to organized T-ball activities.
- Stay open late one day a week to give parents time to run errands.
- Offer parenting classes on evenings or weekends on topics that you feel qualified to teach. Or bring in a professional trainer to teach CPR or first aid.
- Take children to activities sponsored by local religious organizations.
- Buy a caged animal (guinea pig, mouse) and teach children how to care for and raise it. The animal could become your business mascot.
- Specialize by offering only school-age care.
- Have your older children offer to provide evening and weekend babysitting for your clients.
- Specialize by offering care only for children with special needs. If you do this, you could focus your marketing efforts to reach parents through community organizations that serve parents with special-needs children.
- Throw a family picnic in the summer so families can meet one another.
- In December offer to provide evening care so parents can do their holiday shopping. Advertise this service to the friends of current clients and others. December is a time when parents start to think about making new child care arrangements. One provider offered a "Parent Co-op," where she stayed open until 10 P.M. the four Fridays between Thanksgiving and Christmas. Parents who brought their child during these evenings had to work one of the four Friday

evenings. The provider cooked dinner and the parent cared for the children. The parents appreciated the three evenings they could shop, and the provider reported that each gained a new understanding of what caring for a group of children was all about.

If you begin offering a special service, you may be able to identify new places where you could market it to parents. For instance, if you begin offering piano lessons, you could advertise at music schools or talk with music teachers in local elementary schools. If you want to attract more children with special needs, approach the local organizations that serve such children and begin advertising there. If you are offering school-age care, approach your local elementary schools to see if you can distribute your **business flyers.**

Before deciding to offer any of these special services, you may want to survey your current clients to ask for their level of interest. List the special services you are considering and survey the parents: "Are you very likely, somewhat likely, or not at all likely to use this service?" You can attach surveys to payment receipts or hand them out during pick-up time. Even if your current clients are not interested in your ideas, you may still want to offer them in order to attract new clients.

Family child care providers have the potential to meet some of the needs of parents more effectively than child care centers. Specifically, these needs are evening, week-end, and rotating shift care. It is fairly expensive for centers to offer such care because of the high overhead of a building and the uncertain cost of the appropriate number of staff. But family child care can much more easily provide this type of care. Many providers, however, choose not to offer this type of care because of the extra-long hours and disruption it can cause with their own family. There is definitely a demand for this special service, and those providers who choose to offer it are likely to be successful.

Many providers may conclude that they don't have the time or energy to offer any of these special services. It's okay to acknowledge that you already have enough to do. If you do decide to offer a special service, you may need some extra help in caring for the children. Don't allow the quality of your regular care to suffer because of this. Before rejecting the idea of offering a special service, think about what it would take for you and your family to be able to do it. You may find that this can be a source of extra money that will more than pay for your extra work. Parents will often pay significantly more for a special service. Some providers may decide to include some special services in their regular fee and promote them as additional benefits to help keep parents and attract new ones.

Halloween

Why is Halloween a special day for family child care providers? It is the one day of the year that potential clients are knocking on your door! Take advantage of this opportunity to advertise your business:

➤ Put a sign in your window that can be read from the street telling parents about your business ("Preschool Opening").

➤ Invite trick-or-treaters and their parents into your home for cocoa, apple cider, and coffee. If your children's play area is visible from the entryway, turn the lights on in the room so everyone can see what a fun space you have for children. Don't be shy about showing off your space.

➤ Give parents your **business flyer, business card,** and **keepsake**. Encourage them to tell others about your business.

➤ Put your business card and keepsake into the child's candy bag. The parents will find it later. One provider sent me a sample of the business cards that she gave out on Halloween. On it she had taped two crayons that matched the colors on her card. This created a memorable effect.

CHAPTER FOUR

Marketing to Current Clients

One of the first steps in any marketing plan is to keep your current customers satisfied. You want them to stay with you as long as possible because it is far cheaper to keep your current clients happy than it is to attract new ones. Don't ever take for granted that your clients are completely satisfied. Continue to talk to them about what they need. Learn to be a good listener. Ask them how their child is liking your care. Use a **contract update** or written **evaluation** as an opportunity to listen. Keep trying to improve the quality of your program. If parents are happy, they are likely to tell others and give you a favorable recommendation. Parents who are unhappy and pass on negative impressions can hurt your program.

You can market to current clients in a variety of ways, some of which are described in this chapter. Use these ideas to convey the general message to families that the child care services they now receive are worthwhile. You may want to build loyalty by giving rewards to parents who stay with you for an extended period of time. You might offer a free evening (or day) of care for every six months of enrollment.

Ask parents to become more involved in your program as volunteers. Parents can read to children, help out on field trips, prepare activities at their own home and bring them over, make phone calls to remind other parents of upcoming events, copy and mail your newsletter, or help build playground equipment. Some providers ask clients to fill out a Parent Volunteer Checklist at the time of enrollment, indicating ways they might support their program. Some parents may have special skills with a background in accounting, lawyering, advertising, or marketing. If necessary, you could barter care in exchange for some of this help.

Keep the lines of communication open with your current clients. Greet them each day with a smile. Always have something to say at drop-off and pick-up times to share information. At drop-off you may say, "Today we will be playing outside in the sand, where Joshua will learn about measuring and sharing." In the evening, you may say, "Joshua had a lot of fun filling up pails with sand, and he spent time playing with

Cindy and Velissa." More parents leave a child care provider because of poor communication than because of high rates. Do not let conflicts over your **contract and policies** destroy your relationship. Enforce your rules consistently and review them regularly with your clients. Let your current clients know immediately when you will have an opening by writing them a note. Be direct about asking them to pass the word. Offer a **finder's fee,** send flowers, or cook supper for a successful referral.

Use other tools to help you keep in touch with parents, such as a **bulletin board** or a **newsletter.** Other chapters in this book discuss how to approach other providers and organizations to find out more about what parents want, but nothing replaces listening and talking with your current clients every day in order to keep them happy and informed about the benefits of your child care program.

Helping New Clients Feel Comfortable

According to some studies, the time of the highest dropout rate for new clients is six to eight weeks after enrollment. Both parent and child may feel ill at ease for the first few days or weeks after the enrollment in a new program. You can help make this transition period go more smoothly if you take steps to reassure the parent and the child. Here are some ways to help your new clients feel more comfortable:

➤ Shortly after a parent signs up, mail a note or phone the parent thanking him for choosing to enroll his child in your program.

➤ Shortly before the first day of enrollment, send a note to both the parent and child welcoming them to your program. Enclose a photograph of yourself and the children in your care. You may want to include the photo in your **enrollment packet**.

➤ Send the parent a blank cassette tape and encourage her to record herself reading, singing, or talking to her child. Use the tape to help calm the child during the early weeks. If the parent doesn't return the tape within a week, ask the child to remind her.

➤ Ask the parent to bring in family pictures that can be displayed for the child to see.

➤ Have the child bring a favorite toy or nap blanket from home.

➤ If practical, ask the family to bring the household pet for the child to share with the other children.

➤ Create a label with the child's name for a personal space (cubbyhole or special area) to help make the child feel more safe and secure.

➤ Have someone take a picture of you and the child playing with the other children, and give it to the parent for him to post at his place of work. Take pictures (or a video) of the child's first days in your program and place them in a scrapbook to share with the family.

➤ Ask the parent if she would like you to call her at work and let her know how the child is doing, or invite her to call you to "check in."

➤ Make a point of communicating closely with parents by asking them how things are going for them and their child during the first few weeks.

➤ Share with parents that it can take up to two weeks for a child to feel comfortable enough to have an easy transition when the parent leaves.

➤ Invite parents to call any time if they need assurance that their child is adjusting well and feels comfortable.

➤ Invite the parent to drop in at will if he needs assurance that his child's day is going smoothly or the care is what he expects.

➤ If a lot of time has passed between the time of the enrollment interview and the child's first day of care, suggest a 10–15 minute "visit" one or two days before the child begins attending, to reintroduce the child to you and the program.

All of these steps can help you quickly earn the trust of parents and set the stage for a long-lasting relationship.

Bulletin Board

Using a bulletin board is a good way to communicate with the parents of the children in your care. Place the bulletin board where parents will easily see it each morning and evening. Post news such as weekly menus, news of incoming or outgoing parents, upcoming field trips, upcoming birthdays, current newspaper or magazine articles about child care

or child development, your license, training credentials, news of local child care advocacy efforts, announcements of new policies, and reminders of when fees are due. You can also post photos of the children, their parents, and any recent special event. Use the bulletin board to share daily activities and describe to parents what skills the children are learning (see the Skills Children Learn in Family Child Care section in the Appendix). If you receive letters and photos from former clients or children, post them as well.

Periodically, change the content of your bulletin board to keep it current. Throw out old news. Decorate it for upcoming holidays and events. Parents will more often notice your bulletin board if you constantly add and remove items. Your bulletin board should be a source of news and information about what parents can expect from you and what you expect from them. It is a professional way of communicating with parents because it can be used to continually educate parents about the benefits of your program. The more parents understand what you do for their child, the more they will value your service.

Newsletter

A good way to keep in touch with parents is to send them a regular newsletter. Your newsletter can contain

- Weekly menus
- Children's artwork
- Short descriptions of what the children are learning
- Parenting tips (copied from magazine or newspaper articles)
- New policies
- News of any state child care advocacy efforts by your local family child care association or other child care agency
- Introductions of new children and farewells to those moving on
- Current articles from newspapers or magazines about child care issues (If you reprint an article in your newsletter, be sure to ask permission before doing so.)
- Your commentary on stories in the news
- Upcoming birthdays and anniversaries
- Reminders of when payments are due
- Upcoming activities and special events

Your newsletter can be produced on a computer using a variety of type styles and scanned-in photos, or it can be simply designed on a typewriter. If you don't have a typewriter or computer, print your newsletter by hand. To add special touches, you can use clip art found in many software programs or reproduce photographs on a copier and place them in your newsletter. You can also find a lot of free artwork on the Internet. Use different-colored paper each issue or simply add your own color with a marker. Make copies on a copy machine. If your business has a **logo** or tag line, always put it at the top of each issue. Don't worry about trying to produce a fancy newsletter. The most important thing is for your newsletter to look clean, interesting, and readable.

Many providers produce their newsletter once a month, but you can decide whether you want to send one out more or less often. Pick a schedule that is comfortable for you. It is better to start with sending out your newsletter quarterly and then switch to monthly, rather than starting with a more ambitious schedule and then failing to meet your own deadlines.

Send your newsletter to all current and past clients, parents who called or visited your program but did not enroll their child, any parents on your waiting list, and your friends. Everyone who receives your newsletter can help you generate positive word of mouth about your program.

Several commercial parent newsletters are available for providers. They include a variety of activities parents can do with their children. You can pass on copies of these monthly newsletters to your clients or use some of the articles in your own newsletter. Two such newsletters are *Parent Pages Newsletter* (800-531-7526) and *Growing Together* (800-927-7289). Each one is four pages. Call for prices. *Parent Pages* is also available in Spanish.

Birthday and Holiday Cards

Everyone likes receiving birthday and holiday cards. Mail cards to the homes of the children in your care, as well as to their parents. Send holiday cards (Christmas, Kwanzaa, Rosh Hashanah, etc.) as long as you know that the family celebrates the particular holiday. When the child first starts coming, ask the parents what holidays their family celebrates at home and what is an appropriate way to recognize the holiday in your program. Let parents know that you want to share as much of each child's culture in your program as possible. List the children's birthdays in your **newsletter** and on your **bulletin board** so all parents can congratulate the child. Send a card when a client has a new child or adopts. If a child or a relative of the child is in the hospital, send a get-well card. Send a card when a parent does something unusually nice for you or your program. You may also want to send cards for Mother's Day, Father's Day, Valentine's Day, and New Year's Day.

Other Communication

Studies indicate that we communicate not only by what we say, but by how we say it. Most providers have an easy time communicating through speech, so special attention needs to be paid to other communication skills. Putting something in writing can make it easier for the parent to remember. Doing so also creates more legitimacy for your business. Parents are less likely to argue with you if you set out your rules in clear prose. When you want to change a rule or make an announcement, put it in writing and give it to parents. Ask them to read it and tell them you will be happy to answer any questions they might have. Here are some other tips:

➤ Write regular notes to parents describing the child's activities or eating and sleeping patterns. For infants and toddlers, make daily notes. Always find something positive to say about the child. Slip notes in with the children's belongings, pin them to their clothing, or hand them directly to parents.

➤ Take a picture of a new child playing with the other children. Send it to the parents at work. They are likely to post it at their desk where coworkers (and potential new clients) may see it.

➤ If you're going to change any rule in your program, particularly a rule dealing with money or your hours, try to give parents at least a month's notice of the change. Any change to a written contract must be made in writing.

➤ Make copies of newspaper or magazine articles on parenting or child care issues and give them to parents. Ask parents if they have read any helpful article or book that they can recommend. Pass on the name of the book or article to the other parents.

➤ Post pictures of the new families on your **bulletin board** to welcome them to your program.

➤ Give parents a receipt each time they pay you and a summary receipt at the end of the year. Doing so is a sign of professionalism. It communicates to the parent the message that you are running a well-organized business that treats its customers with respect.

➤ The way you dress is also an important way of communicating nonverbally. You want to look professional but not overdressed. Your clothing should be casual and neat. Consider your families as company, and dress as if a casual friend were about to arrive. If you get messy during the day, clean up before the parents arrive. Hang a special apron or smock by the front door to put on if your clothes are messy and parents stop by unexpectedly. You also want your customers' children to look clean at the end of the day. If they have dirty faces or hands, the parent may wonder if the child is receiving enough of your attention.

Finder's Fee

More providers should consider offering a finder's fee to help them recruit new clients. It is a low-cost, no-lose way to get new business. Offer current clients a financial incentive if they refer another parent to you who decides to enroll their child. Don't pay the finder's fee until after the new child has been enrolled for at least one month to make sure the arrangement will last. Current clients are very likely to be selective in whom they refer to you because they will want the new child to be compatible with their child.

You can offer current clients cash, a free weekend of care to allow them to get away, or a week of free care for every successful referral. Offer friends and neighbors a cash reward of an amount that would attract their interest in spreading the word about your program. The amount of a finder's fee can vary considerably by neighborhood. A rough rule of thumb is that it should be at least half of your regular weekly fee. You can also put a time limit on the fee or make it apply only to openings that are harder to fill (preschool rather than infant). Offering such finder's fees is something all providers should consider adopting because you will only pay when you have a successful enrollment. Paying to fill a space in your program is cheaper than virtually any other type of advertising you could do. Offer a finder's fee that is high enough to give someone incentive to take the time to refer your name to someone else. Many child care centers offer a finder's fee program. Find out what the local centers or other homes in your area offer as a finder's fee.

Some providers dislike offering a finder's fee because they feel it is unprofessional. They believe that the idea of giving away any of their time will cause clients to put a lower value on their services. You should make your own decision about whether a finder's fee is a good idea for your program.

Celebrations

Invite the children you care for and their parents to a party at your home at least once a year. It is a good opportunity to interact with clients in an environment that is less stressful than the normal Monday through Friday work week. You could use the party to share with parents some of the positive things that their children are learning, have the children sing songs, or just have a good time. Your party can celebrate a holiday (Christmas, Kwanzaa, Hanukkah, Ramadan, Chinese New Year, Rosh Hashanah, July 4th, Memorial Day) or it could be a backyard gathering in the summer. If you celebrate a religious holiday, make sure your clients also celebrate it. You could celebrate grandparent's day and invite all grandparents to a party.

If you have been in business for a number of years, consider having an anniversary party to celebrate the life of your program. Invite past clients as well. Take pictures of the event and put them in your **newsletter,** on the **bulletin board,** and in your **photo album.** Send an announcement about your anniversary (and a follow-up photo) for the local media to cover. See pages 88–89 for more information about generating media publicity.

If you are celebrating special events or holidays, or are just throwing a party, invite current and prospective clients. You may even want to invite neighbors and friends to help spread the goods news about your program. One provider in Texas told me she has a summer barbecue every year and invites current, former, and prospective clients. Last year more than 150 people attended! This is a marvelous way to promote your program. It allows parents and children to connect with and support one another. It helps to build a community around your program and sends out a message to everyone involved that your service to children is valued and important.

Contract and Policies Update

Family child care providers should have written contracts and policies that they use with their customers to operate their business. Your contract should contain all matters dealing with your fees and hours of operation. These are the things that you can enforce in court. Your policies should contain everything else about how you will deliver your services, including your discipline policy, feeding policy, and sickness policy. You enforce your policies ultimately by terminating your

contract. Your contract and policies should be used primarily as tools to communicate responsibilities and expectations with parents. Conduct a review of your contract and policies at least once a year with parents to make sure that they all understand their roles. Ask parents to explain what each policy and contract term means to them. If their explanation is different from your understanding, change the wording to reflect your intent. If a policy is outdated and no longer relevant, delete it. Add new policies as necessary. Include only those policies you will enforce. You may want to get additional ideas by asking other providers to see what they include in their contracts and policies (see pages 109–111 for a warning about price fixing). The goal of this review is to keep current clients informed and happy and to reduce the likelihood of later misunderstandings.

You should be discussing the progress of each child with parents at least monthly. At these parent conferences you can share information about the child's interests and progress. At least once a year you may also want to distribute a **parent evaluation**. If you don't use a written evaluation, use this opportunity to ask general questions of the parents:

"How are things going for you and your child? Do you have any concerns?"
"Are there any other services you would like me to consider offering?"
"Can you think of ways that I could advertise my program to attract new clients?"

Asking such questions regularly helps you keep in touch with what clients are thinking. It may help you to keep a client enrolled or find a new one. For examples of contracts and policies and an explanation of how they are different, see *Family Child Care Contracts and Policies: How to Be Businesslike in a Caring Profession* by Tom Copeland.

Videotape

Parents often do not have a complete picture of what goes on in your program every day. Some providers periodically videotape parts of their day to help educate their clients. You can use videotapes to show parents how you encourage such habits as reading, physical development, good play skills, helping skills, counting, and brushing teeth. You could videotape special events (birthday parties, holiday parties) or record a typical morning or afternoon activity. For new clients, you could focus on their child for one day. If you have older children, they can help by doing some of the taping, or the older children can direct the entire tape. Get written permission from parents before doing any videotaping (see the Photo, Voice, Web Site, and Video Permission Form in the Appendix). If you don't own a video recorder, borrow one from a friend or customer, or rent one.

You can have the tape playing while parents are dropping off or picking up their children. Doing so allows parents to catch a few additional glimpses of your program in operation. You can offer to lend the tape to parents who want to see more. By making the videotape available, you are sending a message that you want clients to learn more about your program. Whether or not clients borrow the tape, they are more likely to feel reassured that you care. The more parents see what you are doing with the children, the more they will appreciate your program.

Some providers may want to make a more professional-looking tape for prospective clients. Keep it short; 10–15 minutes should be enough. Display your **business name** and phone number on both the tape and the tape jacket. Show yourself interacting with the children. Be sure to get written permission from the parents of any children on the tape. See the Photo, Voice, Web Site, and Video Permission Form in the Appendix. Lend the tape to parents at parent interviews or mail it to interested callers

Evaluations

To help you keep on top of what your current clients are thinking about your program, have them fill out an evaluation form once a year. Your evaluation should be simple. Here are the key questions:
- What do you like best about my program?
- What could I do to improve my program?
- Do you have any other comments or suggestions?

You may want to distribute your evaluation form as part of the review of your **contract and policies**. You should always ask clients who are leaving your program to fill out an evaluation. In this situation add these questions:
- Would you recommend my program to other parents? Why or why not?

When clients are leaving your care, ask them if you can use their name as a reference for prospective clients or use their quotes in your marketing efforts such as a **business flyer**. Put the positive evaluations in a **scrapbook** or **photo album** so new clients can see these written references.

Read all evaluations carefully. Don't worry if you receive some negative feedback. You can't please everyone. If the suggestions are impractical ("stay open till 10 P.M. for drop-in care"), simply tell parents you can't meet this need. If the suggestion is a reasonable one, try to do it. Thank parents for their suggestions and complaints. Tell parents what action was taken to address their complaint. If practical, ask parents for help in monitoring your follow-up to their complaints. A good way to respond to suggestions from current clients is to write a note in your **newsletter** or post it on your **bulletin board**. Look closely at the words parents use to describe the positive aspects of your program.

"Wonderful individual attention to Sally's needs."

"Karen loves to play with all your fun toys."

"I appreciate your flexibility in being able to adjust your hours to meet my work schedule during our busy season."

The positive comments from clients will probably be given in the form of a benefit (see chapter 2). Try to use these phrases in your discussions with prospective clients. For example, "Parents in my program have told me they appreciate the individual attention their children receive and the flexibility in the hours I am available."

Other evaluation questions you may want to include:

- What is the best feature of my program?
- Would you like to volunteer? Doing what?
- How could I advertise my program to attract new clients?
- Are there additional **special services** that you are interested in that I could offer?
- What does your child say about being here?

Many parents may be reluctant to express dissatisfaction with the care their child is receiving. They don't want to offend. They may be frustrated and talk to others about your program without you knowing it. To reduce this possibility, encourage parents to express their frustrations directly to you. Ask them verbally on a regular basis how things are going. Don't rely on a written evaluation as the only way you get feedback from clients.

If you are very sensitive to negative feedback, talk about your feelings with your spouse or a friend. Never complain to one customer about another customer's criticism of you. Do not be quick to terminate a client who voices criticism. See *Family Child Care Contracts and Policies: How to Be Businesslike in a Caring Profession* by Tom Copeland for a discussion of how to communicate and negotiate with clients. Try to learn to accept criticism without feeling personally attacked. Once you have dealt with criticism by changing something (or by deciding not to change!), put it behind you. Let it go and enjoy the new day. See the Appendix for a sample evaluation form.

Some providers use a suggestion box, where parents can give you feedback anonymously throughout the year. You can prepare a suggestion form for parents to fill out that is similar to the evaluation form described above. Some parents may be reluctant to give criticism face-to-face. Handle suggestions from a suggestion box in the same way as described above. Most criticism offered by parents is constructive, because they want your business to succeed, too.

Child Dependent Care Assistance Plans

You should do anything you can to make it financially more attractive for parents to continue coming to your program. For example, you should make sure that all parents participate in a Dependent Care Assistance Plan, if their employers offer one. This employer benefit plan allows parents to set aside a portion of their salary (up to $5,000 as of 1998) to be spent on child care. The amount set aside is not subject to any federal or state income taxes. This represents a substantial tax savings for many families and is usually more beneficial than the child care tax credit. This plan is also known by other names such as cafeteria plan, flexible benefit plan, salary reduction plan, or pre-tax spending account.

Providers should encourage all parents whose employers offer such plans to take advantage of the tax savings. Sometimes parents may not realize their employers offer this benefit plan. The parents should contact their human resources or payroll office for this information. If an employer does not offer this plan, providers should urge parents to talk to their employers about establishing one. It is a simple plan to set up and administer, and tens of thousands of employers, both large and small, now have one. Employers can get further information by contacting a benefits consultant or by asking other employers who have such a plan.

The reason providers want their clients to enroll in these plans is because the tax savings to the clients can filter down to the provider. Parents who get a tax break can often afford to pay more for child care. Under the current rules, a parent can see tax savings of up to $1,400 under this plan. In addition, if the parents don't spend all their money set aside under these plans, they will lose it. Providers should be asking clients to give them any unspent money at the end of the year. You can use this money to buy equipment, open up an Individual Retirement Account, or start saving for some marketing activities! See the latest *Family Child Care Tax Workbook* for a sample form providers can use to ask for this unspent money.

Providers may even want to offer an incentive to clients who sign up for such plans. Offer parents a few hours of free evening care so they can run errands if they enroll or if they get their employer to offer this plan. Some employers pay the provider directly after receiving notification from the employee. Check to see if the employer offers a direct deposit plan so you can be assured of consistent payment.

Money that clients set aside in these plans cannot be carried over and applied to child care expenses in the next year. To keep good records, providers should ask clients to sign a receipt at the end of each year summarizing the child care expenses for the year. For further details on how a provider should handle these plans with clients, see *The Basic Guide to Family Child Care Record Keeping.*

Paid Employees

If you use paid employees to assist you in caring for children, remember that they can help spread good word of mouth about your program. Try to make them aware of the positive aspects of your program and special services you offer so that they can repeat them to their friends and acquaintances. If you use a number of part-time employees throughout the year, keep on good terms with them after they stop working for you. A negative referral from someone who worked for you can hurt your marketing efforts.

Here are some tips to follow for current employees, past employees, and even employees you decided not to hire, to encourage them to refer others to your program:

- Give them several of your **business cards** and ask them to distribute them to possible new clients.
- When you print or revise a **flyer** about your program, send them copies and ask them to distribute some for you.
- Put them on the list to receive your **newsletter.**
- Offer them a **finder's fee** if they refer someone to you who enrolls for several months.
- Invite them to special **celebrations** (holiday parties, summer parties, anniversary parties).

When you hire employees, you can deduct their payroll taxes as a business expense. If you hire your own children under the age of 18, there are additional tax benefits. You do not have to pay Social Security, Medicare, or worker's compensation. Your child may also not have to pay income taxes on this money. See the latest edition of the *Family Child Care Tax Workbook* by Tom Copeland.

CHAPTER FIVE

Low-Cost Promotions

Marketing doesn't have to cost a lot of money or take a lot of time. The ideas in this chapter are inexpensive and easy to do. See chapter 9 for the discussion of how you can afford to pay for marketing. The goal in this chapter is to tell potential clients that your program exists by using inexpensive methods. You start by telling everyone you come in contact with about your business through **flyers, signs, business cards, a welcome mat,** and so on. Some of the ideas in this chapter may not work for you. You may not feel comfortable using all of the ideas listed here. If you are going to try a new idea, follow through on it. It doesn't make sense to buy 250 pencils with your **business name** on them if you don't pass them all out. If you are shy about wearing a **name badge,** maybe you shouldn't get one.

On the other hand, don't reject an idea just because you feel a little uncomfortable. Maybe no other provider in your community uses **incentive coupons** and you feel ill at ease about being the first provider to use them. Maybe one idea seems too exotic or too professional. Don't let this stop you from trying it out. It may work just because no one else is doing it.

Business Name

Because you are a business, it makes sense to operate under a business name. Having a business name is a sign of professionalism. It communicates to your clients that you are serious about your work.

Before using a business name, check on the legal requirements with your state agency (usually the Secretary of State office). You need to register your name only in the state where you do business. If you live near a state border and have clients from more than one state, you should register your name in those states where you draw your clients from. You will probably have to register your business name and pay a small fee (it's tax deductible). Before being allowed to use your business name, your state may check to see that no other business is operating under that name. If you choose to use your own full name ("Maria Garcia's Day Care") you may not have to register it, but if you use only part of your name ("Maria's Day Care"), you may have to register it. Don't be afraid to use your own name as your business name. It's a sign that you are proud of who you are and what you do, and that you deliver personal care for children.

You can choose a professional-sounding name ("The Small School"), or a more child-friendly name ("Country Munchkins"), or a name that tells about your location ("Elm Street Family Child Care"). It's up to you. Depending on your neighborhood, some clients may like a more professional name, while others may not. Some providers want to emphasize the professional nature of their business and use words such as "learning center," "education," "teacher," and "school" in their name. It's your business, so pick a name that you like. (Note: Some states may restrict the use of words such as "school" or "preschool" in your name unless you have a specific type of license. Check with your state child care licensing department.)

Here are some business names of family child care providers from around the country to give you ideas:

Aikoh's Corner	Log Cabin Home Child Care
Bugg House Child Care	Lue's Tiny Tots
Building Blocks Pre School	Mary's Little Lambs
Carney's Angels Child Care	Mr. Mark's Day Care
Country Critters Child Care	Parent Reliever Child Care
Creative Learning Home Care	Rain City Babies (Seattle)
Crok-a-gators	Robin's Nest Family Day Care (provider's
Daycare by Suzanne	name is Robin)
Gramma's Critters Day Care	Safe Haven Child Care
Harmony Child Care Services	Sandy's School Daze
Just Like Home Day Care	Shauna's Tiny Taughts
Lashia's Learning Center	Two-by-Two Child Care
Lil Britches	Tykes 'n' Tots
Little Cherubs	Wee Blossom Day Care

Some providers also use a tag line below their name to help communicate the benefits of their program. A tag line is a way of communicating additional information about your business and distinguishing yourself from your competition. If you have a tag line, use it every place you use your name (**newsletters, business flyers, business card, letterhead, business checks, Web page, keepsakes, enrollment packets, bulletin board, newspaper advertising, T-shirts,** and so on).

Here are some examples of tag lines:

A Home Away from Home

A Loving Home for Child Care

Fun for Children, Peace of Mind for Parents
Let us Maximize Your Child's Potential
Providing Quality Christian Daycare
Quality In-Home Child Care in a Licensed Country Setting
Specializing in: Fun and Learning
The Best Thing to Spend on Children Is Time
We Care We Play We Learn We Grow
We Nurture the Joy in Every Little One
Where Children Explore the World at Their Own Pace
Where Lots of Love Is Put into Quality Care
Your Child's First Teacher

Business Cards and Letterhead

Business cards are one of the most inexpensive ways to promote your business. Your local print shop can make them quickly and cheaply. There is even a Web site on the Internet that specializes in printing business cards for family child care providers (see the Other Resources section of our Web site at www.redleafinstitute.org for more information). Carry them with you at all times and give them away to friends, neighbors, postal carriers, newspaper carriers, workers who make house repairs, and strangers you meet at parties, in grocery store lines, and at the Laundromat. Give two cards to your current clients, so they can put one on file at work. Keep extra cards in your car's glove compartment. Give cards to everyone who is authorized to pick up children (friends, grandparents, other relatives).

If you have a business name, put it on your card. The same goes for any tag line ("A Home Away from Home") or **logo**. You may want to use clip art from software or from your print shop. List your area code along with your phone number. If you have a cell phone, pager, e-mail address, or **Web site**, put these numbers and addresses on your card as well. Some providers choose not to list their addresses for fear that someone who wants to harm children will know where to look. Instead, you may want to refer to the general area you live in ("Crocus Hill Area") or list a partial address ("6xx Portland Avenue") so that clients will know the neighborhood you are in. You can give them the exact address when they call. Be aware that some local telephone companies will give callers the address of any subscriber. You can ask to have this blocked for your phone number. Use the back of your business card to describe your program in more detail. List some of the benefits you offer, such as education equipment available, fun field trips, or special learning programs you use.

Some providers make magnetized versions of their business cards for clients to put on their refrigerator doors or file cabinets at work as a reminder. Because of the additional expense, you may want to give such cards to clients after they enroll with you as a courtesy. You could also buy return address labels (or a rubber stamp) with your business name on it.

Creating a simple letterhead for letters to parents, follow-up notes to prospective clients who call or visit, and your contract can all help to create a professional image. You can find graphics in many computer software programs or use your local print shop. Ask your clients if anyone in their family has computer graphic skills that they would be willing to share in exchange for child care services. Use the same color and typeface design on your business cards and letterhead to maintain a consistent and memorable look. Consider printing up smaller-size paper or self-adhesive notes with your letterhead on them for daily handwritten notes to clients enrolled in your program.

Business Logo

A business logo, although an uncommon marketing tool for providers, can be used to attract the attention of potential clients. It gives your business an additional identity that is eye catching and fun. Your logo can be a picture of something or a graphic design using the letters of your **business name.** It can be taken from a drawing made by the children in your care, or taken from clip art in your computer software. You can have your local print shop or a private consultant design a logo for you. Or you may want to contact your area high school art instructor, who might have a talented student who would design a logo for you for a very small fee. You don't have to make your own drawing exactly to scale. The printer can reduce or enlarge your logo to fit on **cards, flyers, and T-shirts.** Don't use a design or picture copied from a book, magazine, or other published form; it may be copyrighted.

Once you've designed your logo, make sure it complements the style and design of your business card and **letterhead.** If you have a more traditional business name ("Academy of Learning"), don't use a child's drawing as your logo. Use your logo on all of your marketing materials such as your business flyer, T-shirts, **car sign, newsletter, advertising, Web site, keepsakes, name badges, business checks, welcome mat,** and **business sign.** When you do this you will help create a consistent look that will be remembered.

Name Badge

When you are out in the community, let people know what you do. Wear a name badge when you are with the children on a field trip, transporting them to school, shopping at a garage sale, attending a workshop, and so on. You can wear your badge anytime you are engaged in business activities. The most important time to wear a badge is when you are out of your home with the children in your care. If you have employees, they should also wear badges when they accompany you on field trips or other activities. People will stop you and ask about your program. Have a **business card** ready to distribute. The badge should have on it your **business name,** your phone number, and your **logo** (if you have one). To find the names of companies that make badges, look under "Name Plates" in the Yellow Pages.

You also may want to consider having your older children (preschoolers and schoolagers) wear name badges on field trips. The badges should have your business name on them, not the child's name, for security reasons. Parents you meet at the swimming pool or park may be impressed to see the type of activities that children in family child care get to participate in. Name badges can help you spot your children in a larger group more easily and can help raise the visibility of family child care in your community.

Business Sign

A business sign saying "Child Care Available" in the front window of your home may attract people passing by on foot or by car. Some providers put out a lawn sign with their **business name** and phone number on it. Before doing so, however, check with your local government offices to see if there are any ordinances restricting business signs in residential areas. There may be limits on the size and placement of signs or a law that prohibits signs altogether. Keep your sign clean and in good repair. Repaint it when needed. Mow the lawn regularly around the base of the sign. A sign that looks worn reflects badly on your business.

On some special occasions you may want to attach something extra to your sign: when you have an opening ("spaces available" banner), announcement of a **special service** ("second-shift care now available" banner), **celebrations** ("welcome, neighbors" banner for a neighborhood party), or birthdays of the children in your care (attach balloons to your sign). By adding and then removing such announcements, you will attract more attention to your sign.

Warning: The presence of a business sign may also attract the attention of people who may not like the fact that you are doing business in their neighborhood. Sometimes unhappy neighbors may oppose your business (see pages 18–20). You should take this possibility into consideration before calling your local zoning office or putting up your sign.

Business Checking Account and Checks

Although it is not a requirement of your business, many providers have a separate business checking account. When you use checks carrying your business name, people who receive them become more aware of your service. The checkout person in the grocery store, hardware store, or video store, or the pizza delivery person, may be a potential client. Be aware that many banks charge extra for a business checking account.

Whether or not you have a business checking account, you should consider buying checks with a business design on them. The background design can feature a child theme or a more traditional business theme. Your bank may offer such choices or you can buy your checks from companies that sell a wide variety of designs. Often your Sunday newspaper will contain an advertising supplement from such companies. Some mail catalogs also carry such offers.

If you have a **business logo,** include it on your checks. Having a business design enhances the image of your business and attracts more attention from those who receive your checks.

Business Flyer

Providers should have a business flyer or brochure as part of their marketing efforts. The flyer should give a short introduction to your program and motivate the reader to call you for further information. It should be produced professionally at a local copy store or by a graphic designer. Ask your clients if anyone in their family has such a skill and can help you. Most flyers will be no longer than one, two-sided 8½ by 11-inch page. Use bright colors for the paper stock. It could be folded into thirds so it can be used as a mailer. Or you may want to have a flyer printed that takes up half the size of an 8½ by 11-inch page. If you copied your flyer twice on one page, you can print it on heavier paper, cut the page in half, and send it out as a postcard to reduce your mailing costs. You may want to look at other flyers from local centers and homes to get ideas for your flyer. Your flyer should contain the following four elements:

1) Your **business name**, address, and phone number. (Note: Some providers prefer not to list their exact address and include just enough information so parents know the general area. See page 55.) List a nearby landmark to help parents quickly see if your location is convenient for them. Or you can put "near the corner of Grand Ave. and Lexington St." New parents to your community may not know where your specific address is, but their coworkers will probably know where your intersection is. List your phone number in larger type several places throughout the flyer. Identify the best time for clients to call you when there will be the least disruption in your home. If you have a tag line or a **business logo**, include it in your flyer.

2) Three to five benefits of your program. Try to focus on benefits that say something different about your program that will attract attention (see chapter 2). If you offer any **special services**, or have **special educational credentials,** list them here. Don't list your rates because they may change, and you don't want to have to regularly reprint your flyer.

3) Testimonials from parents. Using testimonials from current or past clients can be an effective way to sell your program. Put one or two in your flyer. You may be able to use quotations from old **parent evaluations**. You could also simply ask parents to write a recommendation for you. Most will be delighted to do so. Ask permission if you want to use the parent's quotation or name in your flyer. You may only want to use a first name and last initial. Here's a sample testimonial: "I can't tell you enough how much my daughter Geisha loved coming to your home every morning. Thank you for everything! – Shelly M., mother of a three year old."

4) A graphic design. It is worth the money to hire a professional to design and print your flyer on high-quality paper. You will be handing out hundreds of copies, and you want to make a positive impression on as many people as possible. If you have a **logo**, use it prominently in your flyer. Be cautious about using photographs. They may not reproduce well unless you use more expensive paper stock. Before you use any photos of children, get written permission from

their parents. See the Photo, Voice, Web Site, and Video Permission Form in the Appendix. Drawings or other graphics usually look better than photographs.

Your business flyer should be the primary tool you use to describe your program to prospective clients. You may want to have hundreds of copies of your flyer made to distribute everywhere. Mail copies to parents who call you for an interview. Give them to current clients and any of your employees to distribute to their friends and neighbors. There are many places to distribute flyers in your community (see page 63 for a list of community locations). Ask permission before leaving them at any location. The more professional your flyer looks, the more likely it will be picked up. If you have prepared an **incentive coupon,** you may want to attach the coupon to your flyer.

Provider Web Site

The Internet has created an entirely new way to promote your program. One way to take advantage is to set up your own business Web site. As the number of people who use the Internet continues to increase, more and more parents will turn to it for help in finding child care. If your business is on the Web, you have a greater chance of attracting new clients.

Setting up your own business Web site is easier than you might think. There are books available that describe the process. Many online services (such as America Online and Prodigy) provide such assistance. One Internet site that allows family child care providers to set up their own site for free is located at www.geocities.com/Avenues/Family/Parenting/Child_Care. Geocities can offer this service for free because they will run advertising on your site.

Hundreds of providers have already set up their own Web pages for their businesses. To find out where you can visit these sites, go to www.redleafinstitute.org, click on Other Resources, and check out the listings under Provider Web Sites. You should visit other provider Web sites to get ideas about how they promote their program. In addition to posting some general information about your program and the benefits you offer, you can use your Web site to communicate with your current and past clients. For example, you can post your **newsletter** and any new policies and announcements. You can also scan in photos of the children and their artwork for parents to download or pass on to relatives. Be sure to get written permission from parents before using any photos or artwork. See the Photo, Voice, Web Site, and Video Permission Form in the Appendix. If you establish your own Web site, inform your local **Child Care Resource and Referral** agency so the staff can pass this information on to parents who call the agency. You can also allow older children to send e-mail to their parents at work. Before doing so, ask the parents if this is appropriate. You can also provide links to other parent resources and community organizations.

Because the Internet is still new, it is hard to predict how it will affect the business of family child care. While its impact in the field today may be small, it is likely to grow in significance as time goes on. Providers should pay attention to this new technology by regularly monitoring how other child care programs (homes and centers) and other child care organizations promote themselves on the Internet.

Incentive Coupons

Everyone loves a sale. To attract new clients, you may want to develop a coupon that offers a special introductory discount on your services. Distribute a coupon as part of your **business flyer**, attach them to your **advertisements**, or pass them out like **business cards**. Explore the possibility

$25 OFF

Offer Expires December 31

First Week of Child Care
at
Elizabeth's Happy Tots Child Care
789 Ashland Ave. St. Paul. 651-666-5543

of putting your incentive coupon on the back of receipts from your local grocery store. If this is too expensive, jointly advertise with several other providers and offer one coupon that is good at each program. Put an expiration date on the coupon so you can limit your costs. Coupons should mostly be used as special promotions for a restricted time. You may also want to direct your coupons to a particular audience. For example, offer the coupon only for employees of a company or a church or synagogue near you. Don't offer coupons all the time because it may promote the wrong idea that you are offering a discount service. Here are some suggestions for what to put on your coupon:

- No registration fee
- $25 off the first week of care
- One free evening of care

There are costs associated with redeeming coupons, but usually they are very small compared with the benefits associated with enrolling additional children. Child care centers often offer incentive coupons to attract new business. For some providers, incentive coupons are a sensitive issue. For them, the idea of an incentive coupon conflicts with the professional image they are trying to develop. They would prefer to offer a free evening of care on an occasional basis as a door prize at a local charitable event. Other providers who are trying to fill several openings in a very competitive environment believe that a coupon could be the deciding factor in attracting a parent

Door Hangers

In general, parents prefer a child care program close to their home. Many potential clients probably live close to you. One advertising strategy is to distribute door hangers in your neighborhood. Print a brief description of your program on the door hanger, modeled on what your **business flyer** contains. Print an **incentive coupon** on the bottom of the hanger (with an expiration date). Encourage people who don't need child care to pass the hanger on to someone who might. Use heavy paper stock and have the hanger die cut at a print shop so that it can be hung from the front doorknob. Have your own children deliver the hangers after school and on weekends or hire Boy Scouts, Girl Scouts, or neighborhood children. Make sure they do not put the door hangers in mailboxes. It is illegal to put anything in a mailbox except for mail delivered by the Post Office. Also check to see if there are any local ordinances in your community that prohibit distribution of door hangers. Be aware that some neighbors may not be happy about having a child care program in their community (see pages 18–20). If the door hangers cannot be hung from the front door, put them partway under the welcome mat.

Keepsakes

A major goal of any marketing effort is to get your business name in front of as many prospective clients as possible.

One way to do this is to distribute keepsake items with your **business name** and phone number on it (if you have a **logo**, include that as well). If it is a fun or useful item, the person receiving it will keep it around and others will also have the chance to see your business name. Always be on the lookout for the latest hot item that children or parents are using. Give such keepsakes to your currently enrolled parents and past clients, as well as current and former employees. Mail one to parents who contact you by phone or visit your home for an interview. Pass them out at **Halloween,** parties, picnics, and other gatherings with friends. To find companies that make keepsakes, look in the Yellow Pages or in home product catalogs such as Miles Kimball. Many of these keepsakes can be individualized for children with their name on it as a welcome gift their first day. The following is a list of suggested keepsakes:

Aprons/smocks	Caps/visors	Magnets (in the shape of a
Bumper stickers	Chip clips	house or your logo)
Buttons	Coffee mug	Magnetic clips to hang chil-
Calendars/day planners	Cup holders	dren's artwork on the
Can openers	Frisbees	refrigerator
Canned jam/jelly	Headbands	Mouse pads
Canvas or nylon tote bags	Key chains	Mylar balloons

Notepads
Outlet covers
Pens/pencils
Picture frames

Pins/buttons
Shopping bags/cloth tote
  bags
Soft-foam balls

Stickers
T-shirts (for children and
  parents)
Water squeeze bottles

Distribution of Marketing Materials in the Community

One of the cheapest ways for you to get the word out about your program is to distribute your **business flyer** in locations where parents with young children will see them. You can distribute flyers and **business cards,** post them on walls and bulletin boards, or leave them in waiting rooms and lobbies, or have them run in someone else's newsletters. You may want to attach an **incentive coupon** to your flyer or card to attract more attention. Flyers posted on bulletin boards often get taken down regularly, so you may want to re-post your flyer every few weeks. Some providers attach tear-off slips to their flyers with name and phone number so parents can take the reminder with them. When you distribute your flyers, dress professionally so that you will make a good impression on those you meet. Someone who notices you posting a flyer may be curious and stop to talk. Be sure you have some business cards on hand to distribute. Before distributing materials, get permission from the appropriate person. Some organizations may have rules prohibiting distribution of any advertising.

The more you market your business in the community, the greater the chance you will run into people who don't like family child care in their neighborhood. Because you probably only need to fill a few openings in your program, you may want to start out by distributing only a few flyers to selected locations. Below is a list of some the places you might want to distribute your materials:

Beauty shops
Boy and Girl Scout groups
Child-bearing classes
Childbirth instructors
Children's doctors' and
  dentists' offices
Children's fairs and concerts
Children's toy stores, shoe
  stores, clothing stores
Churches/synagogues
Colleges and universities
  (students, faculty, and
  staff)

Elementary schools (distribute flyers at kindergarten
  open house, where parents
  often are changing
  providers)
Employee bulletin boards in
  hotels and hospitals
Employment offices
Garage sales
Health clubs
House-cleaning services
Large employers (employer
  and employee newsletters)

Laundromats
Libraries
Local businesses
Maternity stores
Midwives
Parenting classes
PTA meetings
Supermarkets
Union offices
Welcome Wagons
Women's organizations
YMCA
YWCA

Welcome Mat

Think of all the people who come to your home: friends, neighbors, postal carriers, delivery persons, children in the neighborhood, salespersons, religious missionaries, survey takers, and so on. A welcome mat on your front doorstep with your **business name, logo,** and tag line on it may result in some of these visitors becoming your next clients. It's an unusual promotion that attracts

attention. Though some people who see your welcome mat may not be likely candidates, they may tell someone else about your business. It even works when you're not at home. Look in home product catalogs or on the Internet (search under "personalized welcome mats") for companies that make customized welcome mats.

Children's T-shirts

When you are out in your community on field trips or just walking around the block with the children in your care, have them wear T-shirts with your **business name** on them. The children will become walking billboards for your business. In addition to your business name, the T-shirts could show your phone number and **logo.** Use a bright color for the shirts, and add a bold design or a children's drawing to attract more attention. Don't put the child's name on the T-shirt, to avoid the potential problem of a stranger walking up to a child and calling the child by name in an attempt to draw the child away from the group. Your business name, however, should be clearly visible.

Parents who see a group of happy children in a public place with colorful, matching T-shirts are likely to be curious and pay some attention. It is not a common sight. You'll be surprised at how often parents will stop to make a friendly comment. Use this opportunity to distribute your **business cards**. Wear your **name badge** as well.

Advertising on Your Car

Many providers use their car or van on a regular basis to transport children to field trips, sport activities, or to and from school. Use these opportunities to advertise your program. If parents see your vehicle, chances are they live close enough to use your program. There are usually no restrictions on placing a sign on your car. Check your local ordinance to be sure. You may want to attach a magnetic sign on the side or back of your car that you can remove later. Or you could attach a paper sign to the inside of your car window (both sides and back). Use a magnetized sign instead of a hand-lettered sign that can easily become worn and yellow. Since passengers in other cars won't have much time to read your sign, keep it simple (Sheehwa's Child Care 614-418-2763).

You could also consider buying a vanity license plate ("Child Care") or a border for your license plate with a message on it ("Family Child Care: The Caring Career"). Order bumper stickers with your name and number (and tag line and **logo**, if you have one) from a local print shop, put one on your car, and give the rest to current clients and friends.

Local Parade

Young children love parades. It's a place where parents and children gather to have a good time. If your town has a local parade, make sure your business is in it. March in the parade with your own children, and invite the children in your care to join you.

You want to be able to keep control of all the children over the length of the parade, so plan to have extra adult help. Don't be afraid to march in a parade with only one or two children. Many parents will be attracted to a small program. Have the children carry balloons and wear **children's T-shirts** with your **business name** on them. Use your double stroller or your wagon to carry the younger ones. Attach a sign with your business name on the stroller or wagon. If you have something special about your program that you want to promote, make an effort to display it. Show pictures of your large play area, computers, special events, or just pictures of happy children. Any decorations, posters, or items prepared with your children to promote the theme of the parade are great advertising. Visuals of what children do in your care are a clear demonstration of the benefits of your program. Bring along **business flyers** and **business cards** to distribute to interested parents you meet. Distribute **keepsakes** along the way.

Alumni Magazine

Have you ever sent a note to your alumni magazine telling them that you are a family child care provider? You should consider doing so if you live close to your college, university, or any other educational institution that you graduated from that has an alumni newsletter or magazine. The best time to send a notice for inclusion in the class notes section is when you have something special to celebrate:

- Notice of your fifth, tenth, or fifteenth anniversary as a provider
- An announcement that you are now caring for several children of other alumni
- Your marriage

Include a photograph of yourself with the children. Sometimes just sending the photograph, with a brief description of what it shows, is enough. You could also send a class note to your spouse's alumni magazine if he or she is working in your business.

CHAPTER SIX

Paid Advertising

The marketing ideas in this chapter are more expensive than those discussed in the previous chapter. Because you only need a small number of clients to fill your program, it may not be wise to spend money reaching tens of thousands of people. It does, however, make sense to jointly advertise with other providers, primarily through your **family child care association.** The cost of advertising can thus be spread over many providers, making it a much more practical option.

Newspaper Advertising

When most providers think of advertising, they think of newspaper advertising. Not every provider can afford to advertise in the local newspapers very often, but it may be appropriate if you are just starting out or have a sudden drop in enrollment. Here are some tips to follow when considering this type of marketing:

➤ Consider where you can advertise most effectively at a reasonable price. Start looking at the choices in your area. These choices might include metropolitan newspapers, neighborhood or community newspapers, shoppers or other newspapers filled almost entirely with advertisements, entertainment weeklies, parent newspapers, union newspapers, and women's newspapers. Look to see if other family child care homes or child care centers already advertise there. You want to place your ad where parents with young children will read it. If the newspaper currently has no advertising from other child care programs, it is less likely that your ad will be noticed. In general, it is better to advertise in local newspapers rather than in large, metropolitan newspapers where your ad may get lost.

➤ An excellent resource to help you decide the best place to run your ad is other providers. Ask a number of providers about their experiences in running ads. Not everyone will have similar experiences, but you may be able to avoid some mistakes made by others.

➤ Once you have identified several possible newspapers for your advertisement, compare their rates for classified ads and display ads. Classified ads are usually four or five lines of copy about your program. Display ads are usually one fourth of page or larger, with graphics. Classified ads are generally much cheaper than most display ads. Usually only centers run display ads because of the expense. But you may want to consider running a one-time display ad in your neighborhood newspaper to announce your opening or the start of a special, new service. Classified ads are usually cheaper during the week and more expensive on Sundays, when more parents read the paper.

➤ Before trying to write your own classified ad, clip out several other ads from homes and centers and examine them closely. You want your ad to be noticed, so don't say the same things that you see in other ads. If every provider in your area is on the Food Program and is certified in CPR and first aid, then it's probably a waste of money to put this in your ad. Notice the language that other ads use. They are probably using words that describe the benefits of their program (individualized attention, computer instruction, professionally trained staff).

➤ Keep your classified ad concise. List your **business name** and tag line (if you have one). Identify the ages of the children you're looking for and any special services you offer (night care, Spanish spoken). Try to stress one or two significant benefits or unique aspects of your program.

➤ Sometimes newspapers will run special advertisement sections or supplements accompanied by short articles on parenting. Call and find out if your newspaper has such a feature. Often such features come out in the early fall. You may want to set aside money (say $20 a month) to be able to advertise with many other programs in this special section. If most of the other programs advertised are centers, then your ad may stick out.

➤ After your ad appears, start tracking how many calls you receive from parents who saw your ad. See the Appendix for a sample Parent Call Tracking Form that you can use for this purpose. You should also be tracking the impact of your other marketing efforts (**business flyers,** networking with other providers and organizations, **finder's fee**) to evaluate their effectiveness. Because the cost of classified ads can add up, you'll want to watch your expenses closely.

➤ After running a classified ad several times, you may want to consider other options. If you received a reasonable number of calls, perhaps you should continue running the ad. If the response was disappointing, perhaps you should consider trying something different. Run the ad on a different day or in a different newspaper. Change the wording in the ad to emphasize another benefit.

➤ Be patient. It is unreasonable to expect a single classified ad to generate enough calls to fill your program. Because parents are only looking for care for a relatively short period of time, your ad has to catch them at the right moment. Newspaper advertising is only one part of your larger marketing effort.

Sample Classified Ads

"Loving, licensed home care provider with structured activities where children have fun learning. Infant and toddler openings. Dale and Summit Avenue. Shaunna 655-XXXX."

"Licensed family child care home open 24 hours Monday–Friday. Experienced staff. Music teacher on site weekly. Spanish enrichment program. School readiness emphasized. A safe, fun learning experience. Chia's Little Tykes in Roseville. 954-XXXX."

"Your child will enjoy our beautiful, large backyard with numerous toys and room to explore. Mother of two looking for preschooler to join small in-home group. Child-centered activities encourage creativity. Lots of TLC. Lynne's Playhouse: 'Learning Every Day, Loving Every Minute.' Northside. 426-XXXX."

Advertising on the Internet

It has only been a few years since advertising appeared on the Internet, but it has quickly grown into a major industry. Although many providers may decide that they can't afford to advertise on the Internet, the industry is changing so rapidly that it makes sense to pay attention to this technology. Here are some opportunities you may want to consider:

➤ Metropolitan newspapers often run classified ads on their Web sites. Check if other centers or homes are advertising here. It's probably the cheapest way to run an ad on-line.

➤ Look for local Web sites that parents may use: parent newspapers and magazines, entertainment weeklies, universities, community colleges, and city guides.

➤ There is a growing number of Web sites for parents looking for child care. In many cases you can list your program for free or for a small fee. Ask your local **Child Care Resource and Referral agency** if it has a Web site and whether you can advertise on it.

➤ If the cost of advertising on the Internet is too expensive, join with other providers through your local **family child care association** and run an ad as a joint project. Your association could also establish its own Web site and carry member ads. The

association could then promote its Web site to parents as a source of information about children's activities and events, parenting tips, and referrals to providers.
➤ There is a Web site at www.careguide.com where you can advertise your program for a monthly fee. Parents across the country can search for child care providers by city. At this time most advertising is for centers.

Television, Radio, and Other Paid Advertising

Here are some suggestions for taking advantage of other advertising opportunities, keeping them within your budget:
➤ Television advertising is generally too expensive for family child care providers. But your **family child care association** can approach your local television stations to see if they run public service announcements for nonprofit organizations. Your association could gain publicity for the family child care field by promoting a special event (clothing drive, relief effort) or by offering a child safety tip for parents. Some television stations offer viewers the opportunity to record a brief editorial viewpoint. Again, work with your association on such a project.
➤ Volunteer to be a supporter of your local public television station during pledge drives. Your **business name** will be read on the air. This is also an activity that your association can participate in.
➤ Some communities have cable access television channels where citizens have the opportunity to appear on a locally produced program. Check out the schedule in your town and see if there is a program about parenting or children. Volunteer to be a speaker. Invite the producers to tape a show at your home. Find out if a television station can tape a special event put on by your association.
➤ Local radio stations, particularly public radio, sometimes run programs focusing on children and parents. Volunteer to be a guest on such a program. If it's a call-in program, don't hesitate to call and voice your opinion. Be sure to identify yourself and your business name. Be a volunteer when the public radio station holds its pledge drive so your business name will be read over the air.
➤ Consider running an incentive coupon in local "entertainment" or "activity" coupon books sold by nonprofit groups as fund-raisers. Perhaps your family child care association could run the ad, with the incentive coupon good in any member's home.
➤ Advertising in the yellow pages is beyond the budget of most providers. It's probably not worth spending your money in this way. Instead, consider having your association run a small ad, promoting its referral service. In some communities, providers must pay extra if they use their telephone for their business. An added benefit, however, is that a yellow pages listing comes with this service, which some providers may consider worth the extra expense.

➤ In many communities there are smaller telephone business directories that carry advertising and compete with the yellow pages. Since most parents do not use these directories, it's probably not a good place to advertise.

➤ Be on the lookout for other opportunities to advertise your program. It may be in publications that parents read, such as a popular local magazine or the public television or radio station magazine. Large employers or local unions may publish newsletters that sell advertising space. Or it could be a special event for children where you give away stickers or other keepsakes. Ask your current clients what they read and where they go to give you further ideas. There are always new opportunities to advertise.

CHAPTER SEVEN

How Other Organizations Can Help

Because providers are often isolated in their own homes, they need to take advantage of every opportunity to network with organizations and individuals that can help them market their business. By working with the organizations identified in this chapter, providers can find out what families want, what services other providers are offering, what age groups and neighborhoods need more services, and what marketing ideas are working and not working. In part, this chapter is about how you can do market research to find out about your customers. For the most part, it costs nothing to contact these organizations and start asking questions. Without having much money to spend on advertising, providers need to spend their time talking to others and asking for help in spreading the word about their program. The most important, and often most underused, organization to work with is your local **Child Care Resource and Referral agency.**

Child Care Resource and Referral Agency

A primary source of free advertising for your business is your local Child Care Resource and Referral (CCR&R) agency. The CCR&R usually maintains and updates lists of all regulated child care homes, centers, nursery schools, and other child care programs in the local community. CCR&R counselors send out names of child care programs to parents who call them. The CCR&R may be housed in a private nonprofit organization or located in a government office. To find out the name and phone number of the agency in your  area, call the National Association of Child Care Resource and Referral Agencies at 202-393-5501; www.naccrra.org (see the Appendix for further information).

The mission of CCR&R agencies is to help parents find child care. If there is not enough child care, they may try to recruit new providers to meet the parent demand. In effect, the CCR&R at times may help to create new competition for your business. It is not a placement service for child care providers. Its job is not to fill your empty slots. Some providers think that all they need to do is get on the CCR&R list and then wait for the parent calls to come. This is a mistake. Managing your enrollment is the key to your business success and this is solely up to you. The CCR&R agency can be a tremendous marketing resource for your business, if you know how to use it. Here are some ways that you can work with your CCR&R agency:

➤ Make sure you are listed on its referral service as soon as you start your business. You may have to meet certain local regulation requirements before your name will be added to the list.

➤ The CCR&R collects information about your program (such as hours of operation and ages of children you will serve) that is used on a daily basis to try to match with parent callers. Make sure your information is current by contacting the CCR&R at least twice a year. Sometimes data about your program can be inadvertently changed on a computer. If your situation changes (your hours have changed, you now have a pet, you now have a toddler opening, or you just received your CDA credential), call immediately to update your file. Don't wait for the CCR&R to call you.

➤ Parents sometimes search for care months before they need it. You may want to contact your CCR&R about your possible future "vacancies." For example, if you know you will have an opening four months ahead, tell your CCR&R about it. The CCR&R will then be able to refer your name to parents looking for care in advance.

➤ Take some time to talk on the phone with a CCR&R referral counselor at least every six months. (Or your local family child care association or network group might want to invite a CCR&R representative to attend your meeting to answer questions.) You can learn valuable marketing information from counselors who are talking every day to parents looking for child care. Here are some questions to ask. The answers to all of these questions can help you greatly in marketing your business:

- What type of care is in the greatest demand in my neighborhood (part-time, infant, special needs)?
- Have any employers near my neighborhood started hiring employees for a second shift or weekends?
- What hours do parents need care for that is now difficult to find?
- Do you have any ideas about what I can change or add to my referral file that would attract more clients?
- Can you give me the names of other providers who are always full that I could contact to ask why they are so successful? (Sometimes the referral counselor may

be able to give you the name of a family child care network coordinator or a mentor whom you can contact.)

- Are any child care centers about to close? (Contact such centers and ask if you can distribute flyers about your program to their clients.)
- What is the range of child care rates (by age group) for homes and centers in my neighborhood?
- What other information do you have about fee policies, vacations, holidays, late fees, registration fees? (Knowing just the average cost of care in your area is not particularly helpful. For a discussion about rates, see chapter 8.)

➤ Ask referral counselors what they tell parents about what to look for in choosing a child care provider. Parents are becoming more savvy in their search for quality care. If you know what parents are likely to ask you, you can better prepare yourself.

➤ Ask the referral counselor if the CCR&R has ever received any complaints about your business. If so, fix the problem, if you haven't already done so. Next, try to find out what impact, if any, this complaint has on how they refer clients to you. If there is a negative impact, see what you can do to reduce the consequences. Clients usually make complaints to the regulatory agency, not to the CCR&R, so they may not have much information.

➤ If you were taken off the referral agency list for some reason (license lapsed, probation), make sure you check to see if your name is back on the referral list once you are eligible to be listed again.

➤ Sometimes providers lose the name of a parent caller and ask their CCR&R, "Who was that parent you referred to me last month?" It is likely that the CCR&R keeps no records of their referrals, so you should remember to record the name and address of all parent callers.

➤ CCR&R agencies sometimes offer training for parents and providers. Find out if you can distribute your business flyer at parent workshops or post it on a bulletin board that parents will see. If you are looking for a part-time substitute or regular helper, post a job announcement on the bulletin board or distribute a flyer at provider and parent workshops.

➤ If the CCR&R publishes a newsletter for parents or providers, ask if you can advertise your business in it. Find out if there are other ways you can promote your services through the CCR&R.

➤ If you can teach workshops on a topic of interest to parents, ask if the CCR&R would sponsor it.

➤ Some CCR&Rs may have a library or other resources that can help your business. Ask about what other marketing assistance is available.

➤ Local media organizations often call the CCR&R asking for names of providers for stories on child care. Tell the CCR&R that you will be a volunteer the next time this happens.

➤ The CCR&R will not give you the names of the parents who called looking for child care in your area. This is confidential information. But they may be able to tell you how many times they gave out your name as a referral in the last six months or year. This can be helpful to know. If you haven't gotten many parent calls and yet your name was referred to a lot of parents, ask why this is the case. You may learn some valuable tips. If you aren't being referred very often by the CCR&R, ask why this is the case.

➤ Some CCR&Rs survey parents to find out why they choose or do not choose providers. The survey might ask how important the following things are to parents in their selection process: **outside appearance of the home,** the provider's manners on the telephone, the cleanliness of the inside of the home, the cost of the care, the number of other children present. If the CCR&R doesn't collect this type of information, you may want to encourage them to do so. Such information can be useful to you in recognizing what's important to your potential clients.

➤ If you find that your local CCR&R is not being helpful to you, or is even showing a bias against family child care providers in the way they administer their referral service, talk to the director of the program and try to negotiate an agreement that satisfies everyone. Your family child care association may want to handle this on behalf of its members.

As you can see, there are a lot of ways in which the CCR&R can help you if you ask for it. It is probably the single greatest resource for your business.

In some communities there are other referral services (commercial and nonprofit) that you may want to contact. Some large employers offer their own referral services. There is also a national child care referral service called The Dependent Care Connection (203-291-3572; Web site: www.dcclifecare.com). Find out if any of such organizations can help you in some of the ways identified above.

Competitors
You are in competition with many other child care programs: regulated family child care homes, child care centers, nursery schools, Montessori programs, legal but unregulated providers, illegal providers, after-school programs, religious programs, employer-sponsored programs, and others. It is a fact of life that your business will always have competitors. But there is a good side to competition that you should take advantage of as you market your business. Here are some tips on how you can learn

from your competition and even cooperate in ways that will benefit both you and your competitors:

➤ To keep in touch with client needs, talk regularly with local competitors about trends, new services, and other changes in the field. You may pick up some ideas that will help your business.

➤ Find out which programs (both homes and centers) have waiting lists and which have openings in your neighborhood. Let those programs who have waiting lists know that you have openings and ask if they will refer parents in your direction. Not all programs will want to do this, but sometimes a program knows that it will not be able to offer any additional infant care (for example) in the foreseeable future and may want to help out parents who call or who are on their waiting list. Be aware that other programs' waiting lists may not be up to date and may not accurately reflect parents who are now seeking care. Some parents may have already found care or will need care sometime in the future.

➤ You should constantly evaluate your competitors, particularly those programs that seem to be successful. Ask yourself, What are their strengths and weaknesses? What special services, equipment, and benefits do they offer that clients seem to want? Why should a client choose my program over competitors? How could I offer something that's slightly different from other programs?

➤ Keep track of the **advertisements** your competitors run in local newspapers and magazines, including ads from centers. Clip them and start a file for your records. Critique each ad, asking yourself, Why does this ad attract my attention? What language does the program use to describe its benefits to clients? How is my program different or similar to this program? If you decide to run an advertisement, review your file for ideas. Often your program has many, if not more, benefits compared with larger centers that advertise heavily. You can use your competitors' advertising to help you focus on what to emphasize about your program.

➤ Identify high-quality programs in your area and arrange to visit them. Most people like talking about themselves and their business. Ask for their opinion about why they are successful. Listen for ideas you can use.

Ways to Cooperate with Competitors

➤ If your programs complement each other (you provide infant care, but not school-age care; they provide school-age care, but not infant care), try to come to an understanding about giving mutual referrals of clients where it's practical. Just because you compete in one area doesn't mean you can't cooperate in another area.

➤ You and your competitor can both enhance your services if you cooperate by sharing activities such as field trips, special events, and celebrations. Share transportation arrangements and use employees to spread the work and have a fun time for everyone. The children will get the benefit of new experiences with different children. You may even want to barter some services, for example, one program hosts the first event and the other program hosts the second event. Use the opportunity of any unique collaborations (particularly between your program and a center) to generate media coverage. Take pictures to share with prospective clients. You can tell your potential and current clients that when they enroll in your program their children will be able to socialize with many other children when they participate in special activities with the local center.

➤ If you would consider offering care for mildly ill children, approach a center that is very close to your home with this idea. Offer to provide temporary care for the sick children from the center for a fee. In exchange, ask the center to give you exclusive referrals or access to some of their services such as a van for transportation. You may even want to start offering specialized sick care services for a number of centers and homes. Before offering any sick care, check with your current customers to see if they have any objections. Also check to see if your child care regulations permit this.

➤ If you use substitutes on an occasional basis as a backup, you may want to share the substitute with a competitor to keep the substitute working regularly and available to both of you.

Family Child Care Associations

All family child care providers should join a family child care association. Most providers live in an area where there is a local association. Some states have a state family child care association. There is also a National Association for Family Child Care (see the Appendix for contact information). Providers should consider joining associations at every level that they can. One of the primary goals of a family child care association should be to market family child care as a service to clients as well as to help providers market their individual programs. Whether the association is a large, statewide organization or a small support group, here are some ways that it can get involved in marketing family child care programs.

Association Benefits

➤ Offer referral services for parents to association members. The association may run local advertisements about this referral service and have a volunteer handle the parent calls. This can be an effective way to spread the cost of advertising. Associations that collect information about provider rates as part of their referrals should be aware of the legal issue of price fixing. Competitors cannot share information with each other about rates. For further details about how rate information can be collected and used, see pages 109–111.

➤ Purchase bulk quantities of marketing materials such as business cards, keepsakes, and name badges to help cut costs for members.

➤ Develop general business flyers for association members such as "The Benefits of Family Child Care" or "How to Choose a Child Care Program." Members could put a sticker with their name and address on copies of these flyers and pass them out to prospective clients. The cost of such flyers would be relatively inexpensive for each provider, and having a consistent flyer in the community promoting family child care would help raise the visibility and image of the field, especially where competition with centers is heavy.

➤ To promote itself, the association can produce its own flyer, "The Benefits of Joining the ABC Family Child Care Association." The larger the association, the more it can do to help its members when dealing with other organizations such as government agencies, **Child Care Resource and Referral agencies,** the media and employers.

➤ Your association can establish its own **Web site** to keep its members informed of legislative changes affecting providers, other resources and services available to providers, training opportunities, and how other providers are successfully marketing their program. Use the Web site to network with other providers.

➤ Last, your association can offer access to tangible services and products through outside vendors, such as insurance (homeowner's, liability, vehicle, disability, umbrella liability), tax preparation services, and financial planning services.

Association Activities

➤ In some states, many child care providers are exempt from state regulations because they only care for a few children. Your association should consider trying to encourage these exempt providers to become part of your association. Many associations currently limit their membership to those providers who are regulated. In the long run, this restriction may not serve the interests of family child care. An increasing number of child care providers are caring for children in their home outside of the regulation system. Associations can reach out to these providers and offer them many services: support, training, access to resources, and more. By doing so, associations can increase their membership and gain greater clout in their advocacy efforts.

➤ Your association should also consider reaching out to illegal family child care providers and encouraging them to become legal. Illegal providers are those who are required by law to be regulated but are not. Once they become legal, you can invite them to join your association in order to take advantage of membership benefits. Find out if there are problems within the regulatory system that make it difficult for providers to become legal. If so, try to make changes by working with local government officials. The association should conduct an education campaign to let clients and illegal providers know exactly when providers must meet local regulations. Use "Tax Benefits of Becoming a Regulated Family Child Care Provider" (see the Appendix) and "The Benefits of Joining the ABC Family Child Care Association" flyer mentioned above to help spread the word. Approach local regulators, the CCR&R, and local media to get support for this educational effort.

➤ For those illegal providers who have received the message that they should stop providing illegal care but have refused to do so, the association could take the next step and report these providers to the local regulatory agency or the Internal Revenue Service (IRS). We are not talking here about exempt providers. We are talking about providers who are required under your state law to be regulated (or licensed) and refuse to do so. This is unfair competition to your program. Such providers are probably not offering a safe environment for children, and the regulatory agency should know about it. Local regulation departments may be understaffed and have little time to enforce the rules. If regulators in your area do not aggressively try to close down illegal providers, you may want to complain to the politicians who oversee their department. This may be a county commissioner or a state representative. When complaining about illegal providers, stress the fact that state and local governments are probably losing tax revenue (because such providers are probably not reporting all of their income), and that they may be liable for injuries to children if they know about an illegal operation and fail to close it down.

➤ You may get more effective action by reporting illegal providers directly to the IRS. The IRS wants to know about those not reporting all income. Make it the job of the association treasurer to check classified ads and notices on bulletin boards and in grocery stores and Laundromats for illegal providers. Association members who hear about such providers could turn over names to this treasurer. The treasurer could contact this person, explain the regulations, and offer help to encourage the provider to become legal. If the person refuses to cooperate after a while, the treasurer could then report these names to the regulatory agency or the IRS. Call 800-829-1040 and talk to any IRS agent. The treasurer doesn't have to know the Social Security number of the illegal provider. Just pass on the name and address. The IRS will keep your name confidential in any investigation. Since the IRS offers a 10% reward of any money collected from an audit based on such tips, this could be an ongoing funds source for the association!

➤ Your association can negotiate with the local Child Care Resource and Referral agency about additional questions when it surveys providers and parents. Ask the CCR&R to collect more detailed information about **provider rates** and reasons why parents choose providers. This information can help with marketing.

➤ Your association can tackle the job of easing local and state zoning laws and home-owner's association covenants to allow family child care in all residential areas. This is a long-term project that would require substantial lobbying efforts, but it is needed in many states. Currently, only a few states have a law that prohibits local city and county governments from restricting family child care providers from running businesses out of their homes.

➤ Associations are the most effective group to lobby on behalf of providers. A group of providers speaking as one voice is more powerful and has more influence than individuals speaking separately. Your association can lobby the government office administrating child care subsidies for low-income clients to speed up payment delivery, or lobby the state to increase standards of quality for all providers.

➤ Finally, your association can work with the local news media to help gain public attention for family child care. Positive media coverage makes it easier for all providers to market their programs. One person in the association should be responsible for making all media contacts. Here are some ideas of association activities that could attract the media:

- Sponsor a late-summer clothing drive for back-to-school clothes for low-income children in your community. Take pictures of association members dropping off clothes at the local Salvation Army or other charity. Ask the radio or newspaper to cosponsor this event.

- Organize a relief drive to provide assistance during an emergency (earthquake, fire, flood). Collect toys, clothing, and food for children of needy families and distribute it through the Red Cross. These types of activities can help make parents in your community associate concern for children with family child care providers.

- Celebrate the anniversaries of providers who have been in business 15, 20, and 25 years. Submit photos of anniversary celebrations to local weekly or daily newspapers, and radio and television stations.

- Organize a fund-raising campaign during Halloween by having trick-or-treaters carry a donation can for a local charity.

At least once a year associations should conduct a survey of its own members to evaluate its own work. Ask what additional benefits and activities the members want the association to focus on. Ask members to prioritize current benefits and activities. The work of marketing to its members should be an ongoing activity of all associations.

In addition to family child care associations, a growing number of organizations, networks, systems, and support groups are organizing to help their members. The largest organization of child care professionals is the National Association for the Education of Young Children (NAEYC). Each state has a chapter. This organization is not primarily focused on serving family child care providers, but some of its state and national conferences have workshops for providers. In some states providers play a more active role. For more information, see the contact information in the Appendix. The largest family child care network is the U.S. military, with family child care systems organized within each service branch. The Head Start program increasingly works with providers around the country. The Child Welfare League of America (202-638-2952) has a family child care system that provides training and other support. Monday Morning America (800-335-4MOM) is a family child care provider management service. There may be other state or local networks or projects in your area. Joining such networks when you can is a way to access resources and support that can help in your marketing efforts.

Child Care Regulators

Family child care regulations vary greatly from state to state. If you have a license or registration system, you probably have a government worker who is responsible for monitoring your program. You may see this person on a regular basis or not. Here are some tips for working with your regulator:

➤ Make sure you keep in compliance with all child care licensing rules. You don't want to give clients a reason to complain about your program. You also want your regulator to speak positively about you when prospective clients call and ask for information about your program. Maintaining a high-quality program starts with following all governmental laws.

➤ Sometimes regulators survey parents who are using your program as part of their relicensing process. Ask your regulator to tell you what kind of feedback has been received from parents. Usually the parents give highly favorable comments about you and your program. If so, you can use this information to help you identify some of your benefits. If some of the comments are negative, yet fair, use the opportunity to identify ways to change your program.

➤ Check with your regulator to see if there are any recorded complaints in the file about your program. Some providers may not be aware that their regulator may have conducted an investigation in response to a complaint. If there has been a complaint against you, and even if the complaint was found to be unjustified, this may be part of your file that is public information. Ask your regulator exactly how any negative information in your file is communicated to a prospective client. You may want a friend, posing as a parent, to call and ask about your record to see what the regulator says about you. Most regulators probably have a lot of leeway in how they share negative information with callers.

Here's an example: Your files may show that there were two complaints made against you five years ago that dealt with a lack of proper supervision. Apparently, a client who was unhappy about having to pay late fees filed a complaint on two different occasions after leaving your program. She told your regulator that you let the children play outside alone while you were preparing lunch. Your regulator investigated and found that you had not violated any rules and no action was taken against you. When a parent calls today, asking about you, your regulator could respond in several ways:

"There are two complaints concerning a lack of supervision in our files."

"There are two complaints concerning a lack of supervision in our files that occurred five years ago."

"There were two complaints made by one person five years ago that were found to be unsubstantiated and we took no action against the provider."

"There is no record of any substantiated complaints ever made against this provider. After three years we do not keep records concerning any unsubstantiated complaints."

All of the above statements are true. Which one the regulator uses can make a big difference in whether the parent calls you for an interview. If you are unhappy about how your regulator responds to parent callers, discuss any concerns you have and make specific suggestions as to how a more balanced picture of your program might be presented. In the above example, you might ask the regulator to always mention that the complaints were unsubstantiated, that they happened over five years ago, and that no negative action was ever taken against you. If you are unable to reach a satisfactory solution with your regulator, talk to a supervisor. It is important for regulators to represent your record fairly. Not doing so can have a significant negative impact on your program.

➤ Ask your regulator for advice about how you might better attract new clients to your program. Your regulator has probably seen many other programs and should be able to point out some ideas that have worked for other providers. Don't be afraid to ask her such direct questions as, "What do you think are my strongest points as a provider? What aspect of my program do you think I should change in order to attract more clients? Do you know how other providers have been successful in attracting clients?" You may be able to use the answers to help you to identify **benefits** about your program.

➤ Ask your regulator for the names and phone numbers of several successful providers who run a quality program and have full enrollment. Call these providers, ask if you can visit them, and talk about why they are doing well.

Food Program Sponsors

Providers who are not already participants should immediately join the Child and Adult Care Food Program in their area. The food reimbursements are a significant financial benefit to your program (see the *Family Child Care Tax Workbook* for details). The nutritious food that you serve as part of the Food Program promotes the health of the children in your care. The Food Program can also be used as a source of marketing support for your program. Here's how:

➤ All Food Programs offer training workshops on nutrition and many also offer workshops on a variety of topics that enhance your business. Attend as many as you can. Talk to other providers about how they market their services and ask what they are hearing about the needs of parents.

➤ A representative from your Food Program sponsor will visit your home at least three times a year to monitor your compliance with the program's regulations. These representatives accumulate a lot of knowledge about family child care as they visit numerous providers each month. Use this opportunity to talk with the representatives.

➤ Ask for tips on how you might improve your business. What do other providers do to market their program? How can you make your program more attractive to clients?

➤ Ask for the names of other providers who offer high-quality care and have a waiting list. Visit these providers to learn more about why they are successful.

➤ Ask if they know other providers who offer **special services.** "What client need do you think exists that I might be able to fulfill?"

➤ Ask the representative if they sense any trends in the child care field. What do they hear from others about new child care programs opening (homes and centers), changes in hiring by local employers, changes in governmental assistance programs for low-income clients?

➤ Your representative will fill out a Home Visit Report Form, which contains information such as how good the food looked, how well the children washed their hands, and the children's manners at the table. You can use this form as a marketing tool to show parents how well you rated by posting it on your **bulletin board** and in your **scrapbook.**

➤ In marketing your program to parents, you should emphasize the nutritional benefits their children are receiving because you are on the Food Program. Because a large percentage of regulated providers are on the Food Program, this does not distinguish you from other providers, so it has limited value as a marketing promotion. In this case, you should emphasize other benefits of your program. If you live in an area where you are competing with a lot of unregulated providers who are not on the Food Program, then it becomes more relevant to stress the nutritional advantages children receive with your program. Your Food Program may also help you with tips on cooking, gardening, and how to use more fresh food.

Government Child Care Subsidy Agencies

Most states have government subsidy programs to help the working poor pay for child care services. Such programs are usually administered by a local governmental unit (usually the county) or in some cases by a private nonprofit agency. Many parents who receive this subsidy use family child care providers. Because the social workers or case managers who work for these programs are in regular contact with many parents looking for child care, they can be a valuable resource for you in the following ways:

➤ Make sure you are eligible to participate in the subsidy program in your area. Check to see if there are any special requirements you must first meet. Get a copy of the rules governing this program so you can find out when to expect payments. Find out whether you can charge clients the difference between what the county pays and what you charge other clients. If you can charge the difference, you should consider doing so. You also want to know whether you can require clients to pay in advance, whether you can receive higher payments if you care for children with special needs, and so on. Although it is a violation of the Americans with Disabilities Act for you to charge clients more to care for children with disabilities, the government can pay you more to care for such children.

➤ Talk to the social worker about how you might attract more clients who receive child care subsidies. Ask, "Do you hear comments from parents about what they are looking for in a child care provider? What can I do to get more low-income parents to visit my program?" Expressing such interest to social workers may influence them to pass on your name to the next parent who comes to their office.

➤ Ask the social worker if there are bulletin boards in the agency's office where you can post your **flyer** or if there are parent newsletters where you can place an ad.

➤ Sometimes the rules governing these subsidy programs can create hardships for providers if they have to wait months before being paid or if parents leave without paying and there is no recourse for collecting the payments from the subsidy program. Providers should talk with the social worker about any problems they are experiencing. If the problem is serious enough, providers may want to work through their family child care association and lobby the government unit for reform. Although at times it can be frustrating to deal with these subsidy programs, providers should think twice before throwing up their hands and refusing to care for these children. Low-income parents can be a consistent source of customers for your business.

Community Organizations

Compared with other businesses, you are somewhat at a disadvantage in marketing your program because you have so few clients. Child care centers, with many more clients, have an easier time generating positive word of mouth. Family child care providers who care for only a few children at a time may have to work harder to market their program. One way to do this is to work with a variety of community organizations to reach prospective new clients.

You want to start getting out the word about your program with organizations where prospective new clients might be found. Or you want someone who works there to tell someone else about your program. See page 63 for a listing of many locations where you can distribute your marketing materials. Below is a listing of the types of organizations and businesses that you should consider approaching.

Churches/synagogues/mosques

Start with your own religious institution, but also stop by the others in your neighborhood. Ask the secretary who gets the calls from parishioners seeking child care and who welcomes new parishioners. Ask if you can post a **flyer** on the bulletin board, put a listing in the church bulletin, and distribute **business cards** at social events and community charity activities, particularly those involving children and parents. Volunteer to work in the nursery school room during services so parents can observe you caring for children firsthand.

Diaper services

New babies will soon need child care services. Distribute business cards, **incentive coupons, keepsakes,** and business flyers through these businesses.

Elementary schools

Visit your local school and talk with the front desk staff. Let them know you are in business and ask if you can leave your business flyers for parents and staff. If you offer sick care, mention this. Some parents may be happy to know there is a provider close to the school they might be able to use. Join and participate in local PTA functions. Your face and name will become more recognizable. Post flyers at kindergarten open houses.

Employers

Start by approaching employers where you already have one employee as a client. Ask if the employer sponsors on-site community fairs or publishes employee newsletters where you could write an article on a parenting issue or place an ad. Some larger employers have their own in-house referral service. Introduce yourself to the staff responsible for running it. Ask if they would give an incentive coupon from you to all new employees.

Hospitals

Maternity wards are great places to distribute **incentive coupons, business flyers,** and **keepsakes.** Ask if the hospital gives out baskets of such items to new parents. Many parents of young children work in hospitals, so you should find out if you can distribute information about your program on employee bulletin boards, in newsletters, or through union activities.

Moving companies/real estate offices

When a new family moves into a neighborhood it can mean there is a need for a new child care provider. Give your incentive coupon or business flyer to these companies in your area and ask them to pass them out to their customers. You may want to offer a free day of child care on moving day for new parents coming into your community.

Obstetrician/Pediatrician offices

Approach these offices near you and ask if they have any health or safety brochures that you could distribute to your customers as a service. Give them your incentive coupons and business flyers and ask them to distribute them to new parents. If you have a special service for babies, highlight this in your materials.

Welcome Wagon

Organizations such as these should be happy to distribute incentive coupons and keepsakes for your business.

Chamber of Commerce

Chambers of Commerce are associations of businesses, and most of their members are small businesses. Since you are a small business, it makes sense to join your local Chamber of Commerce. Here are some ways in which your Chamber can offer you opportunities to market your program.

➤ Most Chambers sponsor regular "get acquainted" gatherings for new members. It is a chance to meet employers who probably have employees needing child care services. Bring plenty of **business cards** and **business flyers** describing your program. Since there will probably be very few other providers who are members of the Chamber, your presence is more likely to attract attention.

➤ Chambers usually offer conferences and workshops on a variety of business topics throughout the year. Although most of them may not be of particular interest, attend several with the intention of learning more about business trends in your community, meeting new people, and distributing your **business cards.**

➤ Find out if the companies closest to your home are members of the Chamber. If so, make a point of introducing yourself to a company representative at some Chamber event. Your chances of being able to distribute flyers at an employer's work site are greatly increased if you establish a business relationship through a professional organization such as the Chamber.

➤ Find out if there are any advertising or marketing agencies or consultants who are members of the Chamber. Approach them through Chamber events and ask them if they ever do any work for small businesses like yours at a discount. Perhaps these companies offer workshops that are open to the public. Some consultants may be interested in helping you or your **family child care association** with such projects as designing a **newspaper advertisement** or reviewing your **business flyer.**

➤ Some Chambers have programs where retired executives offer their services to local businesses or nonprofit organizations for a nominal fee. The Small Business Administration (SBA) has a similar program that is free. Although you may or may not be eligible to receive assistance from this program, your family child care association might be. If so, ask for specific help with marketing-related services. The benefit of this type of program often depends on the particular person involved, so try to do some screening before agreeing to participate.

Generating News Coverage

You may be able to get free publicity if a local news organization decides to run a story or photo about your program. Having a television station, newspaper, or radio station cover your program may not be as far-fetched as it might seem at first. News organizations are always on the lookout for stories, and human-interest stories about children are often very appealing. But you have to have a "hook" to attract the media's interest. That is, you need to have something newsworthy or something that is interesting to view. A story on children learning about farm animals sounds boring. But a picture of young children touching a huge pig can be interesting. Years ago, a child care center in St. Paul got on the local television news by bringing a pig to the classroom.

Here are some possible ideas for stories that you may want to suggest to your local news organization:

- Visits by children to a nursing home to sing songs during the holidays.
- A party celebrating the 20th anniversary of your first day as a provider. Invite a local politician to attend to attract more media coverage.
- A "safe **Halloween**" party at your home where you've invited neighborhood children and have a clown or singer to entertain.
- Special field trips to the state fair or tours of local businesses.

- Pictures of your children in seasonal backgrounds that you submit to the assignment desk at your local newspapers and television stations. Ask the newspapers whether they want photos in color or black and white. Get the written permission of parents before submitting any photographs of their children. See the Photo, Voice, Web Site, and Video Permission Form in the Appendix. Some seasonal ideas include ways to beat a heat wave, building a snowperson after the first blizzard, picking apples in September, choosing pumpkins in October, and taking holiday decorations to nursing homes in December.
- Local history or community celebrations that your program attends, such as Strawberry Days or Founder's Day.
- Flowers that children have planted at local monuments or cemeteries on Memorial Day.
- Picking up litter at your local school playground or park.
- A Bunny-Hop-a-Thon for the Muscular Dystrophy Association.
- An all-green Ring-Around-the-Rosey Marathon on St. Patrick's Day.

If your picture or story appears in a newspaper, make copies and put it in your **newsletter,** post it on your **bulletin board**, add it to your **parent enrollment packet,** and paste it into your **scrapbook**. Make sure you put a caption on the picture or story with your **business name** so that your business will be clearly identified if a parent passes on copies to friends or relatives.

Don't get discouraged if the media don't pick up on your first ideas. Keep trying. Submit pictures or story ideas at the beginning of the month, which can be used later if space is available. Ask news professionals what kind of story they are interested in. Just by introducing yourself, you invite a call for help when the next breaking story on child care comes around.

Handling Negative News Coverage

Occasionally, the news media will write a story about a terrible incident of child abuse or child neglect in a child care home or center. Any negative story hurts all child care programs because it undermines the confidence of parents now using, or considering using, family child care providers. Whether such a negative story originated from a national or local event, you should consider responding to it. You want to counter all negative stories with something positive, or at explain why parents should not fear all family child care. It may be difficult for you to do much as an individual, so it is best if your local **family child care association** can respond to negative news coverage. The following responses will help reassure clients.

➤ Keep your current clients informed about negative news coverage. Write a short note about the news story and post it on your **bulletin board** and in your **newsletter.**

Don't go into detail about the child abuse or neglect. Write about why this incident would not occur in your program. Such reasons might include

- The provider is not regulated. Check with your local **Child Care Resource and Referral agency** to see if the provider is regulated. If not, remind the client that you follow state regulations that make such incidents less likely.
- You have a small number of children that you can easily supervise.
- You have taken training to reduce your stress or you have your spouse or a helper to assist you.
- The incident is less likely to happen in your state because the regulations in your state are tighter.
- You have an open visitation policy with parents.

➤ Ask parents if they have any questions or concerns about a reported news incident. Try to reassure them that you are doing everything you can to protect their child.

➤ Refer parents to other resources that may provide further information (**Child Care Resource and Referral agency** or regulator).

➤ Write a letter to the editor of your local newspaper. Point out why the incident is an uncommon event or why it's less likely to occur in your community. Describe some of the positive aspects of family child care. Some newspapers run guest columns as commentaries on larger news stories. Call your newspaper and volunteer to write such a guest column.

Turn the Negative into a Positive

Whenever there is a negative national news story, even if there has been little local coverage, your **family child care association** should contact your local news organization (television, newspaper, radio) and suggest how the story should be covered locally. If the local television station has already run a story, call the newspaper and suggest a follow-up article. Here are some ideas for how to get news organizations to turn a negative story into something positive:

➤ Encourage the news organization to tell parents where they can get additional resources that can answer their questions and help them become better consumers. The most common sources of such information would be the local **Child Care Resource and Referral agency,** regulatory office, and **family child care association.**

➤ Prepare a flyer such as "How to Choose a Child Care Provider" or "How to Identify Signs of Child Abuse" and offer to send it out free to parents. Approach the appropriate staff at the news organization and ask if they would like to send it out. Offer to put the organization's name on the flyer as a corporate sponsor if they will pay for the printing and distribution.

➤ Refer the news organizations to other sources they should contact for follow-up stories. These could include child development experts, Child Care Resource and Referral counselors, and state child care regulators. These sources may have information about the actual number of child abuse cases that occur in family child care versus in the parents' home. With the rise in the number of children enrolled in child care settings, it's logical to assume that the number of child abuse cases in these settings will grow. But the percentage of such cases probably continues to be very small compared with those occurring in the parents' home.

➤ Tell the news organizations how your local child care regulations compare with those of the state where the original incident occurred. If your regulations are stronger, point out that such cases are less likely to happen in your area. This is the time for a story on the importance of child care regulations and how well they work. If your regulations are weaker, call for their strengthening. Have your association go on record as supporting efforts to change local regulations. Suggest that the media do a story on the importance of stronger regulations and what your state or local government officials are doing about it.

➤ Establish a long-term, ongoing relationship with local news organizations. Offer suggestions for stories on a regular basis (see pages 88–89 for some ideas). Contact the media to cover the annual Week of the Young Child (April of each year), Worthy Wage Day (May 1), and Provider Appreciation Day (the Friday before Mother's Day each year). For further information about these events, see the organizations listed in the Appendix.

➤ Often the media will refer to family child care as "centers." If this happens, call the reporter and point out the correct language that should be used. Television stations sometimes show pictures of a child care center whenever there is a story on child care. Call the station and explain the difference between a home and a center and point out that the majority of children are cared for in a home. Use these opportunities to educate reporters and suggest ideas for positive stories on family child care.

➤ Your association wants to be known as a reliable resource of information on child care issues. Choose one member who will make all media contacts. You want to make it as easy as possible for the media to get information quickly. If your contact cannot answer a specific question, the reporter should be referred to other individuals or organizations.

CHAPTER EIGHT

How to Set Your Rates

In a national survey, parents using family child care were asked, "If your provider asked for $5 more a week, would you be able and willing to pay, or would you look for another provider?" If parents said that they would pay the extra $5 a week, then the survey raised the amount by another $5 a week and kept raising it until the parents finally said they would leave. The results: 71% of the parents surveyed said they would pay $10–$50 more per week to their current provider (see Study of Children in Family Child Care and Relative Care as cited in the Appendix). Does this mean that all providers should raise their rates by this amount? No. It's not that simple.

I have trained tens of thousands of providers across the country on a variety of business issues. I often ask the audience this question: "How many of you have lost a client because you raised your rates?" A few hands always go up. Then I ask, "How many of you with your hands raised now wish you had these clients back in your program?" Virtually every raised hand goes down. The biggest fear providers have about setting and raising their rates is that they will lose the client to another provider. But, in fact, when this does happen providers do not regret their decision.

We will never see a workshop for parents titled "How to Pay More for the Child Care You Now Receive." The responsibility for setting and raising rates will always rest with you. For many providers this is a difficult subject. But it is an important one. Ultimately, your marketing efforts may bring children to your program, but if you aren't charging enough to meet your own needs you may not be in business very long.

How to Think About Rates

Twenty years ago, most family child care providers charged by the hour, charged the same rate for all ages of children, did not charge parents if their child was sick, and did not charge for any vacations or holidays. Today the trend is toward more and more providers charging by the week, charging higher fees for infants than preschoolers, and charging for absences and some paid vacations and holidays. These trends are more pronounced in centers than in homes, and are more common in urban than in rural areas. The main reason for this change is a sharp increase in parent demand for child care and a growth in the number of providers who see their work as a professional career.

Despite these changes, family child care providers generally charge less, and in some cases, significantly less, than rates charged by centers. This difference cannot be explained by the quality of care. Many homes offer higher-quality care for children, especially for infants. The difference cannot be explained by the geographic location of child care programs or by the income level of the clients served. Homes and centers exist side-by-side in all communities, and both serve all income levels. The fundamental explanation for the differences in rates has to do with the reluctance of providers to treat themselves as a business and the failure of providers to market their program as a high-quality source of child care to parents.

Here are some basic guidelines to follow in thinking about your rates. They are not offered as rigid rules. You are free to make your own decision about whether they will work for your program.

➤ The shorter the amount of time you work, the more you should charge for your time. Your drop-in rate should be more than your hourly rate. Your hourly rate should be more than your daily rate. Your daily rate should be more than your weekly rate, and your weekly rate should be more than your monthly rate. Here is a sample rate schedule:

> Drop-in care (not on a regular basis): $3.00 per hour
> Hourly care: $2.50 per hour
> Daily care: $2.35 per hour
> Weekly care (55 hours a week): $115 per week ($2.09 per hour)
> Monthly care (242 hours a month): $423.50 per month ($1.75 per hour)

The reason for this type of rate scale is because it's much more difficult for you to manage your time and make ends meet if parents aren't bringing their child every day, every week. Some other tips:

➤ Charge by the week or month, rather than by the hour. Most providers offer their services for at least 11 hours a day, five days a week. If a parent fails to show up with a child one day, you must still work caring for the other children. Parents are paying you to be available to care for their child every day, whether they use your services or not. Parents often pay for other services even if they don't use them all of the time (apartment rent, magazine and newspaper subscriptions, cable television, and insurance, to name a few).

➤ Charge for days even if the child is absent for reasons of illness, parent vacation, or federal holidays. Most parents work for employers that offer paid time for such days.

Providers need time off to relax and spend time with their own families. Most centers charge for such days.

➤ Require the client to pay up front. Do not provide care unless you have already been paid for it. When you first open your home, ask clients to pay for the first week in advance. If clients currently pay you on Friday for that week of care, here's how to get paid in advance. Clients can continue to pay you on Friday. Ask them to pay you for an extra week's worth of care. If they can't afford to pay this all at once, spread out the payment for the extra week until it is affordable. Most clients could afford to pay an additional $5 a week until the extra week is paid up. Once you get the extra week of payment, the client continues to pay you on Friday, but they are actually paying you for the next week. If clients pay you by the hour, calculate an average weekly payment and ask them to pay this amount up front. If necessary, spread out the payments. Low-income clients who receive subsidies from the government do not control when payments are made. Ask these clients to pay their own co-payment (if any) up front. Offer payment terms if necessary. Advance payments enable you to cover the cost of food and supplies for the week.

➤ Establish a consistent time for payment: day of the week or month, and hour of the day. Set up each client on a payment schedule and stick to it. If a client wants to pay on a Thursday because of family circumstances, and this is acceptable to you, you should consider agreeing to this. A client is more likely to pay on time on a regular basis if the payment schedule fits their needs. You can set up different schedules for different customers.

➤ Require clients to pay for their last two weeks of care up front. When clients finally announce they are leaving, their advance payment entitles them to two free weeks of care, even if your rates have risen since. You do not have to pay interest to the clients on such advance payments. If the client can't afford to pay this all at once, spread payments over a number of weeks or months. Ask clients on subsidy to pay up front for two weeks of their co-payment (if any). Such a policy ensures that you will not be denied payment if a client decides to leave without giving you proper notice.

➤ Consider raising your rates for infants rather than raising your rates the same amount across the board. Infant care is in the greatest demand and family child care providers are more likely to be able to offer higher-quality care for infants than child care centers. Call your **Child Care Resource and Referral agency** to find out how your infant rate compares with other homes and centers.

➤ Consider charging a fee for other services you provide. Examples include late fee, late payment fee, registration fee, holding fee, and activity fee. A late fee reimburses you for overtime work. A late payment fee reimburses you for not getting your money on time. A registration fee pays you for the time spent screening parent calls and interviews. A holding fee pays for your promise not to fill a space with another child, and an activity fee pays for admission and transportation costs on field trips and curriculum costs at home. Sometimes parents just compare weekly or hourly rates in choosing a child care program. Charging separately for these items may make it easier for you to appear more competitive. If you do not charge separately for these fees, make sure you point this out to prospective clients.

➤ Raise your rates every year. Put this policy in your written contract. Providers traditionally resist annual rate increases, and as a result their profit goes down as other costs increase. Raise your rates regularly even if the amount each year is small. Centers typically raise their rates annually.

➤ Consider periodically adding paid days to cover your time when you are closed because of sickness, professional days to attend training conferences, or more vacation time.

Despite all of the ideas just mentioned, it needs to be said that we live in a society that does not provide enough public support for young children. When children are old enough to attend first grade, our tax system offers free education. When students enter a college or university, the cost of post-secondary education is heavily subsidized by government, corporations, and private foundations. In contrast, there are few tax subsidies to help parents pay for preschool education. As a result, many parents have a difficult time paying for high-quality care, and many providers have a difficult time supporting themselves on what parents can afford to pay. Until there is more public support for young children, it will always be hard for providers to earn a living commensurate with the value of the service they deliver to society. Although providers should continue to press for the best possible rates from parents, they should also be advocates in the public policy arena to seek a more equitable child care financing system. The best way to do this is by joining with local, state, and national advocacy organizations, such as the Center for the Child Care Workforce which sponsors Worthy Wage Day on May 1. For more information, see Other Resources in the Appendix.

What Should You Base Your Rates On?

The factors that should determine your rates are the amount you want to earn after your business expenses, the going rate in your community (for both homes and centers), and the ability of clients to pay. Let's look at each one of these factors in turn.

How much do you want to earn providing child care?

Few providers even think of asking this question. Without setting a goal, however, you will probably not reach it. Take the time to think through this answer. What rate is too high? A rate that not enough parents will pay to keep you in business. What rate is too low? A rate that you cannot afford to live on. If you are following some of the marketing tips in this book and are communicating the benefits of your program to prospective clients, you probably should be charging at the high end of the going rate in your community (including what centers are charging). Your goal may be to earn a specific amount of money each year. Or you may want to set your goal to be paid an amount equal to what a teacher in a local child care center earns with the same training and experience as you have. We will use as an example a goal of earning $6 an hour, after business expenses (the current federal minimum wage is $5.15 an hour). Here's how to determine what your rate should be to meet this goal:

1) Calculate your annual income goal

If you are just starting out as a provider, you probably can expect to work about 11 hours a day, five days a week, caring for children, and another 10 hours a week doing other business work like cleaning, record keeping, and meal preparation. This equals 65 hours a week, or 3,380 hours a year (with a two-week, paid vacation). If you have been in business for at least a year, look at line 4 of your previous year's IRS Form 8829, Business Use of Your Home. This represents the total number of hours you said you worked last year. Let's say you have 3,380 hours on this line. Multiply this by $6.00 per hour and the total is $20,280. This represents how much you want to earn after paying for business expenses.

2) Determine your business expenses

If you have not been in business for at least a year, it is difficult to estimate your annual business expenses. There is a worksheet in the Appendix of the latest edition of the *Family Child Care Tax Workbook* that can help you estimate this. A national survey determined that expenses represent about 37% of your income before taxes (see Economics of Family Child Care Study as cited in the Appendix). Using these numbers in our example you would estimate your business expenses at $7,500 ($20,280 x 37% = $7,500). Add this amount to the income goal of $20,280 to determine your actual gross income goal of $27,780. Remember, this goal is just an example. If you have been in business for at least a full year, look at the line titled "Tentative Profit" on your IRS Schedule C Profit or Loss from Business (line 29 on the 1998 form) from last year. This line represents your business profit. We won't include house expenses (property taxes, rent, mortgage interest, etc.) in this total because these would be expenses even if you were not in business. You might want to add to this amount money you want to set aside for retirement or for health insurance. We'll use the $7,500 figure of business expenses for our example.

3) Establish your weekly child care rate

By dividing the income goal of $27,780 by the number of children you care for, you can determine how much you will need to charge per week, per child. Here's the breakdown (assuming a two-week vacation):

2 children ($27,780/2 children/52 weeks) = $267 per week

3 children ($27,780/3 children/52 weeks) = $178 per week

4 children ($27,780/4 children/52 weeks) = $134 per week

5 children ($27,780/5 children/52 weeks) = $107 per week

6 children ($27,780/6 children/52 weeks) = $89 per week

In summary, using this example, if you wanted to earn $6 an hour for your work, you would have to charge an average of $89 per week if you cared for six children, and $107 per week for five children. Many providers are currently charging less than these amounts. These numbers would change if you worked fewer or longer hours and if your expenses were different. You would also need to adjust your rate if you charged different rates for the different age groups. The example also assumes that you maintain full enrollment for the entire year. See the Appendix for a chart of this exercise that you can use to calculate your own weekly rate.

Some parents don't like paying for a provider's vacation because they must pay double for the weeks their provider is gone. You may want to offer parents the option of paying a little more each week so that they won't have to pay you during the weeks you take your vacations. In our example, the provider is earning $390 per week (65 hours a week x $6 per hour = $390). To be paid for a two-week vacation, the provider needs $780. If the provider had two children and each parent paid an extra $7.80 per week, they wouldn't have to pay you during your two weeks of vacation ($780 divided by 50 weeks divided by two parents = $7.80). If you had three children, each parent would have to pay an extra $5.20 per week ($780 divided by 50 weeks divided by three parents). For four parents the amount would be $3.90; for five parents $3.10; and for six parents $2.60 per week.

Remember, this example is not meant to tell providers what rates they should charge. It is intended to help providers better undertand the relationship between their rates and their profit. Six dollars an hour, although more than many providers now earn, is still well below what teachers in public schools earn with sometimes similar training and experience.

If you have been in business for at least a year, here's how you can quickly determine how much you earned per hour last year, after business expenses. Take the number from the "Tentative profit" line near the bottom of your last year's Schedule C and divide it by line 4 on Form 8829. In other words, you are dividing your business profit by the number of hours you worked. Many providers will not be surprised to discover that they are earning much less than minimum wage.

What is the going rate in your community?

Child care rates tend to fluctuate widely, even in small communities. For this reason, it's probably not a good idea to pay close attention to the "average" rate in your area. Your local **Child Care Resource and Referral agency** or **government subsidy agency** can tell you the "average" rate. Ask them when the most recent survey was done. If it is more than six months old, you may want to take into account that current rates are probably a little higher. You want to look at the range of rates to give you a better idea of what clients are paying. Find out what is the range for the highest 20% of rates, and the next lowest 20%. This will tell you a lot. For example, let's say these are the weekly rates in your area for infant care in family child care homes:

Top 20%: $250, 210, 210, 200, 190, 190, 150, 145, 145, 145, 140, 140, 140, 140
Next 20%: $135, 135, 130, 130, 130, 125, 125, 125, 125, 125, 125, 125, 125

This tells us that most of these providers charge between $125 and $150 a week, but there are six providers who charge significantly more. Find out who these providers are and what they are doing to get their rates. Maybe these providers have high fees, but very few infants are enrolled. Or maybe they operate a well-organized, high-quality program that specializes in infant care. It could also be that these providers just decided to charge higher rates and the clients were willing to pay them. Compare yourself to the homes in these two groups to see where you belong. Because the cost of child care varies widely from one part of the country to another, the rates in this example may not be appropriate for your neighborhood.

Now look at the rates of infant care in the child care centers in your area. There are probably fewer centers to gather data on. Just survey those centers that are close enough to you to be your competition. Your CCR&R may have this rate information. Examine these centers to see how their service compares with yours. Are you offering as many benefits? Don't hesitate to compare the quality of your program with that of child care centers.

Conduct the same market research as above for toddler, preschool and school-age care.

What can clients afford to pay?

This factor is the most difficult one to measure. Look at the upper end of what clients could afford to pay. In doing so you may want to set your rates higher than what some clients will pay. There is no rule that says you must set your rates low enough so that no parent will be denied service. It is your decision if you want to keep your rates affordable to low-income parents. But most businesses operate knowing that some customers will not buy their service because of the price. Here are some tips on how to attract and serve higher-income parents:

➤ Offer a special service that few other providers offer. This might mean taking extended field trips or offering music lessons. If clients can't get your service anywhere else, you should be charging a premium price for it.

➤ The hours that you provide care are the most valuable commodity of your business. Consider offering odd-hour care, weekend care, or drop-in care to meet client demand. Ask your local CCR&R agency what hours are the most difficult for parents to find care. When a service is scarce, the price goes up.

➤ Focus on any unique benefits you are currently providing and use them to justify your higher rates. "I speak Spanish, which exposes children to a second language that will help them succeed in school."

➤ If you have never lost a client because your rates were too high, your rates are probably too low. You can never expect to make clients happy when you raise your rates, but many more providers have gone out of business because their rates were too low than because they were too high.

➤ It will probably take more time to find parents willing to pay a higher rate for your services. Your marketing efforts, therefore, should be planned to last longer before you will see results. You should run **ads** and distribute **business flyers** in neighborhoods where higher-income parents live. Your **business name** and the design of your marketing materials should be more professional and less folksy. You may want to promote your program as having a preschool curriculum, describe yourself as a teacher, and charge parents a tuition. This may mean modeling some of the ways in which child care centers create a professional relationship with parents.

➤ Although many providers complain that all clients care about is price, it is probably a myth that clients base their decision primarily on your rates. Parents continue to enroll in child care centers, which usually charge higher rates than homes. Clients are less likely to pay attention to rates when the following circumstances are true:

- You are charging within an expected price range for child care services when compared with other homes and centers. Unless you are at the very high end of rates, this is probably true for you.

- You are offering a service that is valuable at almost any price. Certainly child care meets this definition.

- The service you are offering is desperately needed. This is probably true for infant care and evening care. It is less true for preschool care. Because preschool care is in much greater supply, the price is more competitive and clients will do more price shopping.

- It is difficult for parents to compare their other options with your service. There is little information available to help clients adequately compare one child care program with another. Therefore, parents are less price conscious.

- It is hard to find substitutes to your service. Parents can look in the yellow pages and find a child care center easily. With other options available, price becomes more important.
- Your care seems inexpensive to clients. This is probably not true for most clients.

Because you can relate to most of the statements above, it should mean that parents are not as price sensitive as you might think. Shouldn't parents expect to pay more for a home environment for their child, where there are fewer children and a consistent caregiver who is trained in how to care for children of different ages? Of course.

Talking to Parents about Rates

➤ If you decide to raise your rates, give clients an advance notice of at least one month. This is no time to surprise them.

➤ Don't raise your rates in April (when tax bills are due) or in December (when holiday expenses can be a burden).

➤ September is generally a good time to raise rates because this is when children often leave to begin school and you will probably need to fill an opening.

➤ You can raise your rates only for new clients and keep rates steady for current clients. There is no law that prevents you from charging different rates to different clients based on when the client first enrolled. If you do this you should assume that your clients will eventually find out what others are paying. As long as you have a justification for the different rate, you should be fine.

➤ Don't raise everyone's rates at the same time. If you do, you run the risk of losing more than one parent at the same time. Stagger rate increases so that only one family at a time is affected. You may want to pick the client's anniversary date as the time to raise rates. Note, however, that some providers regularly raise their rates for all clients every January or September without any problems.

➤ Instead of raising rates, you could charge annual fees for liability insurance, attendance at a family child care conference, NAFCC accreditation fees, or other special expenses.

➤ Don't try to over-justify your rate increase. No matter what you say, it may not convince the parent to agree with your reasoning. Just announce your new rates in writing. If clients ask why, tell them.

- My costs have gone up (utilities, property tax, food).
- It is a cost-of-living raise.
- I have another year of experience in providing care.
- I have introduced a new benefit to my program (computer, extra field trips, new curriculum).
- I have taken additional training workshops in the past year.

- I am working longer hours caring for children or preparing activities.
- I am providing certain special services that are not common.
- I will be providing better care for your child this coming year because _____ (fill in your explanation).

➤ Sometimes clients look at what they are paying you each week, multiply it by how many other children are in your care, and conclude that you are making a lot of money. Of course they don't realize all the expenses you have to run your business. To better understand your business, you might want to prepare an income and expense chart like the one below. Lump the business expenses from your tax return into five or six categories as a percentage of your total income. The chart below is based on data collected from family child care providers in three cities for the report "Economics of Family Child Care" (as cited in the Appendix):

Income	Average (1992)
Parent fees	90%
Food Program	10%
Total gross income	100%
Expenses	
Food	35%
Employees, insurance	26%
Supplies, toys	17%
Professional fees/other	10%
Maintenance/repairs/equip.	7%
Transportation/gifts	5%
Total expenses	100% (37% of gross income)
Profit	63% of gross income

Note: The expenses do not include taxes or house expenses (property taxes, mortgage interest, etc.) that existed before the business began.

This chart shows that the average provider in this study kept only 63 cents on every dollar of income earned. Your financial chart may be very different. The point is that most providers must spend a lot of money on business expenses to operate successfully. When you are thinking about how much money you are making, you should always be looking at your profit, after business expenses. You may want to share some of the information on your own financial chart with your customers to help educate them about your business. Maybe you just want to share a couple of expense categories such as food and supplies/toys. You don't want to share this information as a sole justification of your rates, but many parents will be surprised at how much you must spend to stay in business.

➤ Don't argue with clients who say your rates are too high. They may be too high for the particular client you are talking to. You may want to mention ways in which your fees could be considered more affordable by pointing out the benefits of the federal child care tax credit, **child dependent care assistance plans,** any discounts you offer for second children, or any other special discounts you might offer.

➤ Your best way of communicating about your rates is to talk about the *value* of your service, rather than the price. The cost of providing quality child care is expensive. Parents can always find cheaper care somewhere else. You should continue to point out how the benefits of your service will help their child and that your rate takes this into account. Clients will pay more if they can see the value of your benefits and the quality of your service.

➤ Parents sometimes believe that if child care costs more, then it must be worth it. A few years ago a parent called a **Child Care Resource and Referral agency** looking for care for his infant. After getting several names from the referral counselor, the parent asked, "Which provider charges the most?" The counselor started to explain that he should check out all the providers and compare their services, when the parent interrupted to say, "You don't understand. I want to know who charges the most, because I think that provider will offer the best care." Parents, like many consumers, believe that they get what they pay for. Parents generally pay more to enroll their child in a child care center because they believe they are getting higher-quality care. In part this belief is based on the higher rates charged by centers. If you are charging less than a center and claiming that the quality of your care is better, some parents may wonder why you aren't charging more. When you price your work, you price your worth.

➤ Parents are reluctant to change their child care provider and are more likely to pay you an additional amount rather than be inconvenienced and search for another provider.

Everything in this chapter about setting rates applies even if your client is a relative or someone who was a friend before enrolling with you. Although you have a personal relationship with relatives and friends, you must still establish a business relationship when dealing with money. You should clearly set out your rate schedule and enforce it in the same manner. If it feels too uncomfortable to be in a business relationship with a relative or friend, then you should reconsider what you are doing. You may feel more comfortable providing care for free, or you may decide that you would rather not provide the care at all.

In the end, you deserve to be paid as a professional provider who is doing the important work of teaching young children and helping them develop into adults. You are worth it! It's up to you to do something about it.

CHAPTER NINE

Other Marketing Issues

This chapter addresses some key issues that arise in marketing family child care.

Competing against the Fancy Child Care Center

A new child care center has just opened in your neighborhood. It cares for 100 children (toddler through school-age) and has a well-equipped playground, a van to transport children, and sparkling classrooms with bright furniture and plenty of toys. You start to feel desperate thinking that now you'll never fill your two openings. "How can I compete?" you wonder. Here's how:

➤ Visit the center and get copies of all materials they are distributing to prospective clients: rate schedules, statements of philosophy, description of the program's benefits, special services offered, and time-limited special discounts. Watch for any advertisements that the center may be running in local newspapers, or magazines, or in flyers distributed in the neighborhood. (See pages 109–111 about how to collect this information without violating antitrust laws.) You want to keep monitoring what this center is doing. Prospective clients who call you may be comparing what you offer with what this center offers, so you need to be informed.

➤ Look over all the material you have collected. Think about how your program is different. Look at your benefits. What do you offer that this center does not? Your answer might contain some of these benefits:
  - Smaller group size for more individual attention for each child
  - Home environment where children can play in familiar, comfortable surroundings
  - Home-cooked, individually prepared meals
  - Healthier environment for children because there is less illness in a small group of children
  - More convenient location

- Lower cost (Although some providers may want to market themselves using this benefit, readers of this book should by now understand that many providers can successfully compete on the basis of the quality of their care, not lower rates.)
- Longer hours
- Years of experience, giving children a consistent caregiver (Center staff usually turn over quickly, resulting in a less stable relationship between caregiver and child.)
- Mixed age groups, allowing siblings to be together
- Transportation to and from school, or a school bus stopping at your home
- Credentialed or accredited provider

Remember, your program may never have everything this center offers, but you will always have some benefit that a center does not have. See chapter 2 for a description of how to identify the benefits of your program.

➤ Call your **Child Care Resource and Referral agency** and ask what type of care is in greatest demand in your neighborhood. You may want to adjust your program to offer second-shift or weekend care, or to focus on caring for children with special needs or of different ages than you are currently caring for.

➤ Distribute **door hangers** and **business flyers** in your neighborhood that describe your program, identify your key benefits, and offer a discount on the first month of care.

➤ Offer current clients a **finder's fee** if they refer a parent who enrolls with you.

➤ Work with your local **family child care association** to run some advertising in neighborhood newspapers. The ad should promote family child care and give a number to call where referrals can be made to homes in your neighborhood.

➤ Introduce yourself to the director of the center. Suggest ways in which you might cooperate. Since this center doesn't offer infant care and you do, ask if it will refer parents with infants to you (or to your family child care association referral service). Offer to provide backup care for the center for mildly ill children. Offer to provide drop-in care if a client needs care until 7 P.M. but the center closes at 6 P.M.

Competing against Informal Caregivers

They are popping up everywhere: providers who run their businesses outside of the regulatory system. They are either exempt from regulations because they care for only a few children, or they are operating illegally. The best way to compete against illegal providers is to turn them in to your local government regulators or to the IRS (see page 80). But what can you do about the increasing number of providers who are not operating illegally, but operate without having to follow all of the regulations that you must?

➤ The number one concern of parents about child care is safety. You should, therefore, emphasize to parents that being regulated means you and your program have passed a series of safety tests, including criminal background checks on all adults in the home, first aid/CPR training, fire department inspections of your home, and adherence to safety standards, such as storage of hazardous materials around the home. Parents who use an informal caregivers must check these things out for themselves to ensure their child's safety.

➤ Informal caregivers probably charge less, perhaps significantly less, than you charge. Do not try to compete on the basis of price by lowering your rates. There will always be providers with lower rates. You can be successful without undercutting your competition. Think of the hotel industry. There are cheap hotels and expensive hotels. They all compete in different ways to attract customers. As a reader of this book, you should probably not see yourself as a Motel 6 or Super 8. How about an Embassy Suites or a Sheraton?

➤ You can compete against informal caregivers by stressing the value clients receive from your services. You do this by promoting the benefits of your program as described in chapter 2. What advantages do you offer children and parents who enroll with your regulated program? You might answer as follows:

"I offer a variety of planned learning and play activities that will help your child be ready to succeed academically and socially in school."

"I have a backup caregiver who can provide care if I am ever sick or gone, so you won't miss work."

"I have specialized training in child development, so I can respond quickly to your child's needs."

"I offer special services (piano lessons, second-language training, numerous field trips, computers) that will enrich your child's education."

If clients can see what they are paying for, most will pay for higher-quality care. You can't hope to appeal to everyone. Some parents will always pick the cheapest care. Let those parents go. People usually get what they pay for. Parents who pay bargain-basement rates will get bargain-basement care.

➤ Work with your **family child care association** or **Child Care Resource and Referral agency** to initiate a public education campaign about the benefits of regulated child care. Direct this campaign at both parents and informal caregivers. To parents, stress issues of safety, training, and professional care. To informal caregivers, stress the benefits of the Food Program, access to support, and the ability to earn more money by caring for more children. See Tax Benefits of Becoming a Regulated Family Child Care Provider in the Appendix.

Marketing to Clients Who Have Left

Who knows your program the best? It is probably the parents and children who have been a part of your program and now have moved on. Don't forget this population as a target market. These clients are likely to retain a very positive feeling about the care you provided. You want to encourage them to tell others about your program. Word of mouth is so critical because personal recommendations carry a lot of weight in the field of child care. Prospective clients will listen to the advice of friends and co-workers. Here are some suggestions for how to promote your program through former clients and their children:

➤ Always try to be on good terms with clients when they leave. Tell them they are welcome to return. Ask them to fill out an **evaluation form.** Send them a thank-you note shortly after they leave. There is a possibility that the parents will not like the new child care program and will want to return.

➤ Send them several copies of your **business card** and **business flyer** and encourage them to distribute to other parents.

➤ Keep sending your **newsletter** to these parents so that they will continue to feel a part of your program.

➤ Continue to offer a **finder's fee** if they refer a parent who enrolls with you.

➤ Send them a New Year's card with an update about your program for the past year.

➤ If you are looking for financial help in purchasing some new equipment (swing set, computer), ask past clients for a contribution. Or ask parents to donate old toys or equipment to your program. Put a list of items you need in your **newsletter.**

➤ Encourage parents to send you pictures of their children as they grow older and write you letters describing how the children are doing. Post such photos and letters on your **bulletin board,** in your **scrapbook,** and in your **newsletter.**

➤ Continue to send **birthday cards** and graduation cards to the children. As the children grow up, establish a direct correspondence with each child. Encourage children to continue to write to you and send pictures of themselves.

➤ Continue to use these parents as references.

➤ Continue to send **holiday cards** to past clients. Invite them to your special **celebrations.**

The longer you stay in business the more important it is to maintain a lasting relationship with parents and children after they leave your care. The measure of the success of what you do for children in your program is how well they succeed in life after they leave your program. As these children grow up, you want to use their progress as examples to show prospective clients that how you run your program works.

Prospective clients will come to your home for an interview and probably share some different views on child discipline, teaching techniques, religious faiths, and child-rearing philosophies. You can reassure these parents that they need not fear for their child about any of these differences if they enroll with your program. Do this by pointing out that you've cared for many other children of parents like them, and that these children are turning out fine. ("Billy's in high school now and on the swimming team. I got a letter from him last month and here's the picture he sent along of himself at a swim meet.") Pictures and letters from former clients and their children are powerful statements of how well you did your job. Parents who see this ongoing connection that you have with the families in your care will understand that these are the important things in life, not the small differences you might have today. Parents will want to be a part, along with their children, of this lifelong relationship.

Price Fixing: Collecting Information About Rates

What do the following situations have in common?
- At an association meeting or training workshop, family child care providers discuss how much they charge clients.
- In order to find out the going rate in her neighborhood, a new provider calls another provider and asks what she charges clients.
- A **family child care association** surveys its members about rates and shares the results at the next association meeting.

In all of the above situations, there is a probable violation of the federal antitrust law. What's going on?

Federal antitrust law says that it is against the law for competitors to discuss their rates with each other. The law is designed to encourage competition and discourage competitors from setting prices higher than they would be otherwise. When providers discuss rates at association meetings or training workshops, this can easily be construed to be a discussion to raise rates. This is true even if there are no direct statements made encouraging providers to raise rates.

Many providers and family child care trainers are not aware of how federal antitrust laws affect the family child care field. Although this law is regularly violated when providers discuss rates over the phone, providers should be most concerned when the issue of rates comes up at association meetings or training workshops.

It is important for providers to be informed about what other programs (homes and centers) are charging. This information can be used to help you market your program. If you are charging less than other programs, you can promote this as a benefit. If you are charging more, you can promote the value of the other benefits you offer that justifies a higher rate. Be careful about how you use the rate information you do collect.

If your rates are higher than the "average" in your area, don't assume that this means you must lower them to be competitive. Also, don't assume that you shouldn't raise your rates either. Your rates should be based on what you want to earn and the cost of doing business. See chapter 8, How to Set Your Rates, for more information. How can providers collect rate information without breaking the law?

➤ If you call another provider or visit a child care center, don't identify yourself as a provider. Both parties must know they are competitors for it to be price fixing. Say you are a parent looking for child care and you want to know what local rates are. Or you could have a friend visit the center, collect information about rates, and bring it back to you.

➤ Look at classified ads and **business flyers** posted in your neighborhood to see what other providers are charging.

➤ Call your local **Child Care Resource and Referral agency** or local **government child care subsidy program** and ask for any rate information it has collected. Many CCR&Rs and government agencies conduct regular surveys of provider rates (homes and centers). You can ask for this information as a provider without fear of breaking the law. Rate information can be shared if it meets these three tests:

1) The individual or organization must collect the rate information and make it readily available to the public.

2) The information must be communicated in such a way as to not allow anyone to identify the rates of any one provider.

3) The sample of providers surveyed must be large enough so that no one can identify the name of any one provider.

➤ Usually the CCR&R or the government agency collects only minimal information about rates (average cost of care by age group). Ask the agency to collect additional information that is more useful, such as

- Range of rates (lowest third, middle, highest third)
- Range of rates for
  —Providers open less than two years
  —Providers open more than 10 years
  —Providers who are members of the association
  —Providers who have a CDA or are NAFCC accredited
  —Providers in a close geographical area to your home
  —Percent of providers who charge for these services and the range of costs:
    –Provider vacation
    –Parent vacation
    –Registration fee
    –Activity fee

–Late pickup fee
–Late payment fee
–Bounced check fee
–Second child discount
–Holding fee (maternity leave, summer break)

If the CCR&R or government agency surveys providers for this information and shares it with the public (which includes parents who call looking for child care), then individual providers can receive it.

Members of family child care associations should also be concerned about how they collect rate information. Associations who operate their own referral service for parents and collect specific rate information from their members can give this information to parents who call, but they cannot share this information with other providers in the association. If your family child care association wants to collect rate information from its members, it must follow the three tests identified above. That means the association would have to have someone, besides a provider (who is a competitor), collect the information. In addition to passing out the rate information to parents, the association could calculate the average rates for its members and make this information available to the public. This could be done by sharing the results with the local CCR&R and government agencies or by publishing the results in local parenting magazines. By sharing average rate information with the public, association members could then have access to this data. Associations can always share rate information collected by CCR&R agencies or by government agencies with its own members.

How Can I Afford to Pay for Marketing?

Marketing your business doesn't have to be an elaborate campaign or cost a lot of money. But a successful business will have to spend some money on marketing. Many of the ideas in this book are very inexpensive. Plan to spend a few dollars each month on your marketing efforts. Remember that all of your marketing expenses are 100% tax deductible.

On the following page is a list of the top 10 low-cost marketing tips for your business. If you are starting out or need to fill an opening and you don't have much money, try these ideas first. If you follow all 10 ideas, they would cost you probably less than $200 a year, or about $15 a month. The costs are estimates. They will vary in different parts of the country.

Top 10 Low-Cost Marketing Tips	Estimated Cost
1) Choose a name for your business and register it with your state. (See pages 53–55.)	$30
2) Print up 250 business cards listing your name and phone number. Distribute your cards to friends, relatives, neighbors, and others. (See pages 55–56.)	$15
3) Create a one-page flyer about your business. Identify three things about your program that are special and put them in your flyer. Print and distribute 100 copies at local businesses, churches, and schools. (See pages 58–60.)	$25
4) Record a friendly and professional greeting on your answering machine or voice mail that identifies your business and invites parents to leave a message. (See pages 20 –22.)	0
5) Place a four-line classified ad in your local community newspaper. (See pages 67–69.)	$25
6) Talk to your local Child Care Resource and Referral Agency about being a part of its referral service. Ask a referral counselor for tips on how to attract clients. (See pages 73–76.)	0
7) Join your local family child care association and take advantage of its member benefits. (See pages 78–82.)	$25
8) Offer a finder's fee to anyone who refers a parent to you who enrolls and stays at least three months. (See pages 46–47.)	$50
9) Clean up the outside of your home and your entryway so that it creates an inviting and safe first impression to parents. (See pages 17–18.)	0
10) When a parent calls about your program, make sure you follow up with a thank-you note and a return call to try and schedule an interview. (See page 32.)	$.32
Total Estimated Cost	**$170.32**

CHAPTER TEN

Evaluating Your Plan

Child care is a dynamic service industry that has just come of age as a profession. Marketing is a year-round, ongoing process. Here are some final tips to help you with your marketing efforts.

➤ Marketing should be fun! Promoting your business shouldn't always be a deadly serious activity. Try to laugh at yourself as much as possible and have a good time, whether you are marching in a **local parade**, throwing a holiday or **Halloween party**, passing out balloons, or writing the next issue of your **newsletter**. If you're not enjoying yourself in your business, you should find something else to do that will make you happy.

➤ Marketing needs attention over the long run. Pace yourself. Don't do six activities the first month and then nothing for the next eight months. See the Annual Marketing Calendar in the Appendix for ideas about how to schedule your activities.

➤ All of your marketing activities should support each other. This can be done if you have a consistent message with the same look. You should continually promote the benefits of your program to prospective clients. The benefits should consistently appear in all of your written materials (**business flyer, classified ad, door hanger, Web site**). Use the same color and design on all your marketing materials.

➤ In addition, all of the other marketing tips in this book should work together to help define your program. You may have a brilliant business flyer, but if your telephone manner is unfriendly, parents will turn away. Or you may be very successful in enrolling new clients, but if you can't communicate with clients about their needs you probably won't keep them for long.

➤ Don't rely on any one marketing idea to fill your openings. Don't assume that you only need to tell parents once about your program. You will probably have to use different marketing messages repeated several times before a potential customer will listen.

➤ Try not to become overwhelmed by the many ideas suggested in this book. Pick out a few to get started. We don't expect you to use all of these ideas. And don't be afraid to try your own ideas.

➤ At least once a year, take time to evaluate your marketing plan. Here is how you can review your efforts:

- What am I doing to keep my current clients happy?
- How well is it working?
- What ideas have current clients suggested that I can implement now?

➤ Look at your current clients and see if you can identify any similarities: where they live, their ages, jobs, lifestyle. How did they hear about you? Knowing this information may help you in focusing your marketing efforts for the coming year. Consider the following questions, as well:

- How did parents who call me hear about me? Which marketing ideas worked? What other ideas should I try now? What ideas are working for other providers?
- How many parents who contacted me ended up enrolling in my program? Why didn't more enroll?
- How many parents stayed with me? How many parents left in the past year? Did I provide all of the benefits I said I would in my marketing materials?
- What advice do these organizations have to help me: **Child Care Resource and Referral agency, family child care association**, and **child care regulator**?
- What can I learn this year from my competitors?

➤ For some providers, marketing can be stressful. If you are feeling anxious, take a step back and don't initiate any new marketing activities for a while. To help avoid burnout, take a Friday off or take a vacation. Seek help from a support group or a mentor. There will probably always be times that you will need some extra help to reduce your stress level.

➤ Be patient. Few marketing efforts produce instant results. It takes time to build a successful business.

➤ Appreciate yourself. Be proud of your commitment to help young children. Your work is important and you shouldn't feel shy about promoting what you do. If you decide that you can't meet your business goals and have to quit, don't be discouraged. Your business may have failed but you have not. As long as you have a positive attitude about yourself, you will succeed.

Appendix

Annual Marketing Calendar

Marketing is a year-round activity. Don't try to squeeze all of your efforts into a few months. Try to maintain a steady stream of activities each month. The cumulative effect of your marketing will grow over time.

Here's a sample list of marketing tasks spread throughout the year. You can follow this schedule or establish your own. Post your schedule where you will see it regularly, such as in your office.

January
Call your CCR&R to see that your listing is correct and talk to a referral counselor about parent demand.

Offer current clients a finder's fee if they refer a parent with a preschooler to your program who stays enrolled for at least three months.

Fill out the IRS W-10 Form and give a copy to each parent. Have the parent sign a year-end receipt for last year's child care payments. Mail a copy of the W-10 to those parents who left you earlier in the year. Send past clients a copy of your business flyer.

February
Identify three benefits of your program. Post them next to your phones.

Register your business name with your state.

Give your current families a Valentine's Day card and a note of appreciation.

March
Print business cards and distribute at least 30 to friends and neighbors.

Record a new greeting on your answering machine.

April
Knowing that you will lose a toddler when a parent moves out of town in June, call your CCR&R to tell them you will have an opening for a toddler shortly.

At the family child care association meeting, ask for the names of two providers who have waiting lists. Talk with them about why they are successful.

Anticipate how many school-age openings you will have for the summer and tell your CCR&R.

May
Set (or raise) your summer rates now so parents have adequate notice. Reevaluate your vacation pay policy for parents who leave in the summer but plan to return in the fall.

Distribute 100 door hangers in your neighborhood.

Locate at least three provider Web sites on the Internet. Write down three marketing ideas you could use.

Send a thank-you card to current and past clients for Mother's Day.

June

Update your contract with parents.

Distribute 50 business flyers at local businesses.

Send a thank-you card to current and past clients for Father's Day.

July

Conduct a clean-up project for the outside of your home. Plant flowers in the front.

Start a newsletter for parents.

Conduct a local park cleaning with your children. Send photos and an article to your local newspaper.

August

Call your CCR&R to update your listing and talk to a referral counselor about parent demand.

Start a photo album showing off your benefits.

Run a classified ad in your neighborhood newspaper.

September

Raise your rates by 4% over the next three months.

Send to the grandparents of your children a card with their photograph for Grandparent's Day.

October

Throw a Halloween party and invite the neighborhood children. Distribute your business flyers or business cards to trick-or-treaters.

Write an article on "Safe Trick-or-Treating" for your local newspaper. Give copies of your article (written on your business letterhead) to parents and ask them to distribute copies to their friends and coworkers.

Attend a workshop on child development.

November

Join the Chamber of Commerce.

Put a business sign on your van.

December

Run a classified ad in a different neighborhood newspaper.

Identify one new benefit you will add to your program for the next year.

Hold a holiday get-together for your current customers.

How Much Do You Want to Earn?

A Table to Calculate a Weekly Rate for Parents

    _____   Enter the hourly rate you want to earn.

X _____   Enter the number of hours you work in a year (include such hours as cleaning and record keeping). Use line 4 from your IRS Form 8829.

= _____   This is your gross annual income.

+ _____   Enter your annual business expenses. Use line 28 from your Schedule C.

= _____   This is your net annual income.

Enter the number of children you want in your care and the number of weeks you want to work in a year.

_____   _____   _____

Net annual income ÷ Number of children = *Annual income per child*

_____   _____   _____

Annual income per child ÷ Number of weeks worked = *Weekly fee to charge parents to reach your hourly rate goal*

Parent Call Tracking Form

Date of call _____

Name of parent(s) _____   _____

Address _____

Phone # _____ home _____ work

E-mail _____

Name of child   _____ Birth date _____

                              _____ Birth date _____

                              _____ Birth date _____

Desired start date _____ Rate quoted _____

Any special interests or needs of the child: _____

_____

_____

How did you hear about my program?

    ___ Flyer: where did you pick it up? _____

    ___ Sign on my lawn

    ___ Classified ad: name of newspaper _____

    ___ Child Care Resource and Referral agency referral

    ___ Referral from an individual: name _____

    ___ Other: identify _____

Parent concerns/notes: _____

_____

_____   _____

Date interview scheduled _____

If par~nt declined interview, why? _____

If I turned parent down, why? _____

Parent Interview Checklist

Date of interview _____

Name of parent(s) _____   _____

Address _____

Phone # _____ home _____ work

E-mail _____

Name of child   _____ Birth date _____

                          _____ Birth date _____

                          _____ Birth date _____

Desired start date _____ Rate quoted _____

Parent references:

    Name _____ Relationship _____ Phone # _____

    Name _____ Relationship _____ Phone # _____

    Name _____ Relationship _____ Phone # _____

How does the parent show an interest in the child's behavior during the interview?

_____

Does the parent show a willingness to be flexible and adapt to my rules?

Yes ___ No ___ Any problems

Signs that the child may be difficult to care for _____

_____

Does the parent treat me with respect and have a positive attitude? Yes ____ No ___

Comments _____

Questions raised by the parent that concern me _____

What do I like about this family? _____

What concerns do I have about this family? _____

Skills Children Learn in Family Child Care

Activity	Specific Skills Learned
Finding toys or learning materials to work with alone or with others	Cognitive: Makes decisions about interests and abilities. Self-help: Finds toys by himself or sets up environment for play. Social/language: Learns to share, barter, manage conflict, and ask for help. Emotional: Learns about acceptance and rejection. Expresses needs.
Block play	Cognitive: May count blocks, sees pattern and design. Learns to build and plan structure. Matches blocks that look alike. Social: Learns to share and cooperate. Physical: Learns to balance blocks and line them up (small motor coordination).
Dramatic play	Cognitive: Decides appropriate dress and appearance for roles; uses visual perceptions to assess self, others, and play environment. Learns and remembers behaviors to imitate. Develops abstract thinking abilities. Social: Plays adult roles. Develops self-image and coordinates with others. Learns to express feelings. Language: Learns to express self in another role.
Setting the table	Cognitive: Counts silverware, glasses, and napkins, or places one object by each setting Follows pattern of place settings. Knows which is soup spoon or salad fork. Social: Cooperates with other children. May teach younger children to help. Physical: Picks up and places objects (small motor coordination).

Sitting down to eat	Cognitive: Measures to pour. Understands directions. Social/language: Learns appropriate table conversation and manners. Physical: Pours milk, passes the dish (small motor coordination).
Story time or listening to music	Cognitive: Listens and retains information. Follows storyline (sequencing) with eyes and/or ears. Recognizes words, pictures, instruments, and rhythms.
Fingerplays and songs	Cognitive/language: Learns words, gestures, and melody (sequencing, repetition, speech, and listening skills). Follows directions. Physical: Coordination (small and large motor) for gestures and finger plays.
Dance	Cognitive/language: Listens to music and rhythms. Learns to understand simple movement directions and their relationship to the music. Physical: Coordinates movements (large motor).
Climbing/riding	Cognitive: May count the rungs to the top of a climbing structure; plans climb. Maps out direction and distance to ride; watches for others in path. Social: Takes turns, interacts. Physical: Large motor coordination, balance.
Sand play	Cognitive: Measures sand and maps out roads (spatial relationships). Social: Shares, interacts, cooperates. Physical: Pours, dumps, pushes, gathers, scoops, packs (small and large motor).
Putting away toys	Cognitive: Sorts toys, follows directions. Social: Takes turns, learns to handle toys carefully. Physical: Places object on the shelf, replaces lids, opens and shuts doors.

Taken from *Family Day Care* May/June 1990

Choosing Child Care Checklist

Choosing Child Care Checklist
Provider _____
Date program was contacted _____
Address _____

_____

Phone number – home _____
Phone number – work _____
Ages of children now enrolled, not
    including the provider's own children _____
Ages of provider's own children _____
Hours open _____
Cost per hour/week/month
    infant _____
    toddler _____
    preschooler _____
    schoolager _____
Other fees
    Enrollment fee _____
    Number of yearly paid holidays _____
    Number of yearly paid vacation
    days taken by parent _____
    Other _____ _____
Special services offered _____

_____

Key benefits of the program _____

_____

_____

Training credentials _____

_____

References _____

Top Five Signs of Quality to Look for in a Child Care Program
- A small group size
- A program focused on meeting the child's needs
- A safe place for children
- A program where there are lots of fun things for children to do
- A provider with training in child development

Enrollment Form

_____ (*Parent name*) hereby agree to enroll their

child_____ (*Name of child*) with the

_____(*Name of program*). The first day of enroll-

ment will be _____ (*date*). Provider promises to begin providing care for
this child on the first day of enrollment.

Parent will pay an enrollment fee of $ _____ that will hold this spot until the
first day of enrollment. This fee is due at the signing of this form. This enrollment fee
is nonrefundable, whether or not the parent brings the child for care. Parent will sign
and return the provider's contract on or by the first day of care.

_____   _____

Parent signature   Date of signature

_____   _____

Parent signature   Date of signature

_____   _____

Parent signature   Date of signature

Waiting List Form

1) Name of parent(s) _____
Address _____
Phone # _____ home _____ work _____
E-mail _____ Date placed on waiting list _____
Name of child(ren)   _____ Birth date _____
                       _____ Birth date _____
                       _____ Birth date _____
Desired start date _____ Rate quoted _____
Notes _____
_____

2) Name of parent(s) _____
Address _____
Phone # _____ home _____ work _____
E-mail _____ Date placed on waiting list _____
Name of child(ren)   _____ Birth date _____
                       _____ Birth date _____
                       _____ Birth date _____
Desired start date _____ Rate quoted _____
Notes _____
_____

3) Name of parent(s) _____
Address _____
Phone # _____ home _____ work _____
E-mail _____ Date placed on waiting list _____
Name of child(ren)   _____ Birth date _____
                       _____ Birth date _____
                       _____ Birth date _____
Desired start date _____ Rate quoted _____
Notes _____
_____

4) Name of parent(s) _____

Address _____

Phone # _____ home _____ work

E-mail _____ Date placed on waiting list _____

Name of child(ren)   _____ Birth date _____

_____ Birth date _____

_____ Birth date _____

Desired start date _____ Rate quoted _____

Notes _____

_____

5) Name of parent(s) _____

Address _____

Phone # _____ home _____ work

E-mail _____ Date placed on waiting list _____

Name of child(ren)   _____ Birth date _____

_____ Birth date _____

_____ Birth date _____

Desired start date _____ Rate quoted _____

Notes _____

_____

6) Name of parent(s) _____

Address _____

Phone # _____ home _____ work

E-mail _____ Date placed on waiting list _____

Name of child(ren)   _____ Birth date _____

_____ Birth date _____

_____ Birth date _____

Desired start date _____ Rate quoted _____

Notes _____

_____

7) Name of parent(s) _____

Address _____

Phone # _____ home _____ work

E-mail _____ Date placed on waiting list _____

Name of child(ren)   _____ Birth date _____

_____ Birth date _____

_____ Birth date _____

Desired start date _____ Rate quoted _____

Notes _____

_____

Sample Press Release

PRESS RELEASE

FOR IMMEDIATE RELEASE   DECEMBER 28, 2000

FOR MORE INFORMATION CONTACT:
OWNER LI'L DARLINGS 223-XXXX

LOCAL CHILD CARE PROVIDER FEATURED IN GRAND AVE PARADE

This year the annual Grand Avenue New Year's Day Parade will feature children from The Li'l Darlings Family Child Care Home. The five children from the four families enrolled in this child care program will be dressed in hand-made costumes matching the parade's theme, "From the Frontier to the New Age."

Roberta Darling, the owner of Li'l Darlings, says she wanted her children to partici-pate in the parade because "it will be a fun activity for the children. They have worked very hard over the past two months to plan their costumes and decorate the wagons they will be pulling." Darling's program was chosen as one of the three new parade participants selected each year by the parade committee.

Li'l Darlings is a licensed family child care program that has been in operation for three years. It is located on Portland Avenue near Laurel Street. Li'l Darlings serves children from ages six weeks to six years. Roberta Darling recently earned her early childhood development degree from Concordia College.

Parent Evaluation Form

1) Overall, how would you rate the care I provide your child? Circle one.

Needs Improvement		Pretty Good		Wonderful
1	2	3	4	5

2) What do you like best about my program?

3) What could I do to improve my program?

4) Would you recommend my program to other parents? Why or why not?

5) Would you like to volunteer in my program? Doing what?

6) How could I advertise my program to attract new clients?

7) What additional "special services" are you interested in that I could offer?

8) Other comments or suggestions:

Parent's name (optional) _____ Date _____

Child's name (optional) _____

Photo, Voice, Web Site, and Video Permission Form

Waiver and Release

I/We hereby consent to the use of the voice or the likeness in photographs or on videotape of _____ (*name of child*) by the _____ (*name of child care program*) in the production of any business flyers, newsletters, Web sites, voice mail messages, videotapes, and any other advertisements or promotions that _____ (*name of child care program*) may decide to develop, now or in the future.

I/We also hereby agree to waive and forego any right or entitlement of claim I/we might have to any compensation, fees, or other benefits except for a waiver fee of $1.00.

Further, by signing this waiver and release I/we certify that I/we am/are the legal parent or guardian of the child identified above.

Parent/Guardian _____

Parent/Guardian _____

Date _____

Tax Benefits of Becoming a Regulated Family Child Care Provider

This chart shows how three providers with identical expenses can have a very different net profit depending upon whether the provider is regulated or a member of the Food Program.

	Unregulated or Illegal Provider	Regulated or "Exempt" Provider	Regulated and Food Program	Fill in your estimate
Income				
Parent fees				
(5 children x $70 per week)	$18,200	$18,200	$18,200	_____
Food Program – Tier II				
($165/month for 5 children)	0	0	1,980	_____
Total Income	$18,200	$18,200	$20,180	_____
Business Deductions				
Advertising	100	100	100	_____
Business interest	20	20	20	_____
Office expense	750	750	750	_____
Supplies	1,000	1,000	1,000	_____
Laundry/cleaning	50	50	50	_____
Food	2,800	2,800	2,800	_____
Dues, books	100	100	100	_____
Training expenses	100	100	100	_____
Household items/toys	700	700	700	_____
Helper	100	100	100	_____
Car expenses	372	372	372	_____
Depreciation on $8,000 of appliances and furniture	400	400	400	_____
Utilities ($700 x 35% T/S†)	*	245	245	_____

House depreciation ($62,000 home x 35% T/S† over 39 yrs)	*	534	534	_____
Homeowner's insurance ($300 x 35% T/S†)	*	105	105	_____
Mortgage interest ($3,000 x 35% T/S†)	*	1,050	1,050	_____
Property taxes ($600 x 35% T/S†)	*	210	210	_____
Total Deductions	6,492	8,636	8,636	_____
Taxable Income (Income – Deductions)	11,708	9,564	11,544	_____
Social Security Tax	1,654	1,351	1,631	_____
Federal Income Tax	1,756	1,435	1,295	_____
Gross Profit (Taxable Income – Taxes)	8,298	6,778	8,618	_____
House expenses (marked above with a *) that are not deductible	- 2,144	- 0	- 0	_____
Net Profit (Gross Profit – House expenses not allowed)	**$6,154**	**$6,778**	**$8,618**	_____

†T/S means Time-Space percentage. See *The Basic Guide to Family Child Care Record Keeping* for more information.

*These are not deductible for unregulated providers.

It is a federal law that child care providers earning money by caring for children in their home (whether licensed, regulated, exempt from regulation, or illegal) must report their income to the IRS. Many providers do not report their income either because they aren't aware of the tax laws or because they are worried that they will owe too much in taxes. This flyer is designed to show how all providers can significantly reduce their taxes. For federal tax purposes, a child care provider falls into one of two categories:

1) A provider who is required to meet but does not meet state regulations (such as licensing or registration) is called an unregulated or illegal provider. Although the author does not recommend being unregulated, such providers should be aware that they can take many business tax deductions if they report their income. See column one of the chart. Taking deductions can greatly reduce any taxes owed.

2) A provider who does meet state regulations is called a regulated provider. A regulated provider is entitled to claim house expenses in column two (house depreciation, insurance, mortgage interest, property taxes, and utilities) that an unregulated provider cannot claim. A provider who is exempt from state regulations is entitled to all the same deductions as a regulated provider but is usually not eligible to participate in the Food Program. Regulated providers can increase their net profit by joining the Food Program (see column three).

Besides claiming additional tax deductions, there are many other benefits of becoming a regulated child care provider. You can

- Join the Food Program and be reimbursed for some of your food expenses.
- Obtain liability insurance to protect your business.
- Join a local association of family child care providers and receive the benefits of membership.
- Sign up to be listed by your local **Child Care Resource and Referral agency,** which will refer parents to your business.
- Attend training workshops and receive other support services.
- Become eligible for local grant and loan programs in some areas.

Notes on the chart: The numbers in the chart are only estimates shown for comparison purposes. Your income and expense will vary. Not all the business deductions or tax consequences are shown on this chart. We used a 35% Time/Space percentage (T/S) representing the portion of the home used for business. We used a 15% federal income tax rate. Notice that the deductions are the same for each provider, except that the unregulated provider cannot claim expenses associated with the house. By losing these deductions, this provider pays more taxes. These deductions (totaling $2,144) are subtracted from the unregulated provider's gross income because the provider had to pay these expenses anyway, even though they are not allowed as a business deduction. Also notice that an exempt provider (one who is not required to meet local regulations) can claim all of the same deductions as a regulated provider. The provider on the Food Program pays more taxes but has the highest net profit. Every provider is better off by joining the Food Program.

Other Resources

Organizations

Center for the Child Care Workforce
733 Fifteenth Street NW, Suite 1037
Washington, DC 20005
202-737-7700
www.ccw.org
Sponsors the Worthy Wage Campaign and Worthy Wage Day (May 1). Publications on wages and working conditions include "Creating Better Family Child Care Jobs: Model Work Standards," and "Who's Caring for Your Child? Critical Questions."

Child Care Law Center
973 Market Street, Suite 550
San Francisco, CA 94103
415-495-5498
www.childcarelaw.com
Publications about the Americans with Disabilities Act (ADA), as well as other publications about zoning, contracts, and other legal matters.

Council for Early Childhood Professional Recognition
2460 Sixteenth Street NW
Washington, DC 20009
800-424-4310 phone
202-265-9161 fax
www.cdacouncil.org Web site
Information about the Child Development Associate (CDA) credential.

Head Start
www2.acf.dhhs.gov/programs/hsb
A child development program that has served low-income children and their families since 1965.

Monday Morning America, Inc.
Monday Morning Moms ®: A Family Day Care Management Service Franchise
800-335-4MOM
www.mondayam.com
A family child care provider management service

National Association for Family Child Care
525 SW Fifth Street, Suite A
Des Moines, IA 50309
515-282-8192 phone
515-282-9117 fax
nafcc@nafcc.org e-mail
www.nafcc.org Web site
Information about local associations, newsletters, and accreditation programs. Also has a family child care marketing kit available for purchase.

National Association for the Education of Young Children
1509 Sixteenth Street NW
Washington, DC 20036
800-424-2460 phone
202-328-1846 fax
www.naeyc.org Web site
Membership information, publications, and training.

National Association of Child Care Resource and Referral Agencies
1319 F Street NW, Suite 810
Washington, DC 20004
202-393-5501 phone
202-393-1109 fax
www.naccrra.net Web site
Information about how to contact your local CCR&R agency, and publications.

Provider Appreciation Day
888-3-FIRST-1
www.providersfirst.com
An annual day of appreciation for all child care providers celebrated the Friday before Mother's Day.

Studies

"The Economics of Family Child Care Study" by Kathy Modigliani, Wheelock College, and Suzanne W Helburn, John R. Morris, and Mary L. Culkin, University of Colorado, Denver, 1992. Unpublished.

"The Study of Children in Family Child Care and Relative Care" by Ellen Galinsky, Carollee Howes, Susan Kontos, and Marybeth Shinn (New York: Families and Work Institute, 1994).

Family Child Care Marketing Guide Feedback Form

We are very interested in receiving feedback from readers of this book regarding your experiences in marketing your business. We will share this information on our Web site and in the next edition of this book.

- What marketing ideas have worked best for you?
- What one tip would you recommend that a new provider follow to attract parents?
- What new areas of marketing information should the next edition of this book cover?

Send your feedback to our Web site (www.redleafinstitute.org), or call us at 651-641-6626, or write us at Redleaf National Institute, 450 N. Syndicate, Suite 5, St. Paul, MN 55104.

We appreciate hearing your ideas that will help other providers.

CALENDAR-KEEPER™ SOFTWARE

For use with Windows 95, 98, ME, 2000, and NT

The complete business management software for child care professionals

For more than twenty years, Redleaf Press has been providing the best in business essentials for family child care providers. We've worked with a team of industry professionals, including Tom Copeland and Redleaf National Institute, to offer the most comprehensive and easy-to-use software for the business of family child care. We are proud to offer *Calendar-Keeper* Software, the solution for family child care providers.

Calendar-Keeper Software is the most complete software system ever created and designed specifically for family child care and group home providers. Order today and enjoy these benefits!

Family and Child Information - Complete record keeping includes contact information, medical information, emergency contacts, allergies and special care instructions, attendance, and immunization history with due-date reminders. The "Flextracking" system allows unlimited user-definable tracking for files such as child incidents/accidents, medications, and parent meetings. You can even scan emergency contacts and pictures of parents and children into each record!

Income/Receivables - Track all child care income quickly and easily with automatic billing and simple account maintenance. Print a receipt as soon as payment is entered, parent statements, even the actual IRS W-10 for each parent at the end of the year.

Expenses and Mileage - Extensive expense records are kept easily with prebuilt tax and expense categories. Time-Space percentage and business-use percentages are automatically calculated and applied for tax reporting. Mileage log maintains all business-related trips and automatically records mileage for trips to vendors when the expense is entered. Simply click and print worksheets for Schedule C and Form 8829 at tax time.

Meals/Menus - Designed for providers on or off the Food Program. Create meals and menus easily using a preloaded list of food items that can be added to or modified. The system even verifies that the menus meet CACFP requirements. Track meal counts and rotate menus for a complete solution.

Extensive Reporting - Print out all information with total flexibility, including more than 80 reports to choose from!

Includes articles, advice, and business tips from Tom Copeland, director of Redleaf National Institute and the leading national authority on the business of family child care. Also includes activities, recipes, nutrition tips, and more.

30 Days of Free Technical Support • Annual Updates Available for Purchase

For a free demo visit www.cksoft.com

Visit
www.redleafinstitute.org

The Web Site of Redleaf National Institute
The National Center for the Business of Family Child Care
Contents of the Web Site:

- Special pages for Members of the Institute

- Latest news on tax and business issues

- Question and Answer section

- Business Library of IRS Tax Court cases, legislative news,
  articles by Tom Copeland, and more

- National Tax Preparer directory

- Information about training workshops around the country

- IRS audit assistance section

- Special resource section for family child care associations, child care resource
  and referral agencies, child care food program sponsors, and family child care
  military coordinators

- Plus listing and links to other family child care business resources

Also from Redleaf Press

REDLEAF BUSINESS SERIES

Buy the entire **Redleaf Business Series** for your family child care business!

Family Child Care Record-Keeping Guide
The only complete guide to record keeping for family child care providers. Lists more than 1,000 allowable business deductions.

Calendar-Keeper: A Record Keeping System Including Nutrition Information for Child Care Providers
This guide helps you organize all your income, attendance, and expense records by month. The best record-keeping calendar available!

Calendar-Keeper **Software: The Complete Business Management Software for Child Care Professionals**
Visit www.cksoft.com for more information or for a free demo.

Family Child Care Contracts and Policies
Includes sample contracts and policies and how-to information on using them effectively to improve your business.

Family Child Care Tax Workbook and Organizer
The complete resource on how to do your taxes for your business.

Family Child Care Inventory-Keeper
A handy guide filled with lists of what you can claim for depreciation for your taxes.

Family Child Care Mileage-Keeper
This mileage log book for vehicles you use in your business shows exactly how to keep the proper records to claim business expenses.

**For a free catalog or more information
call toll-free 800-423-8309 or visit www.redleafpress.org**